STENCIL·TYPE

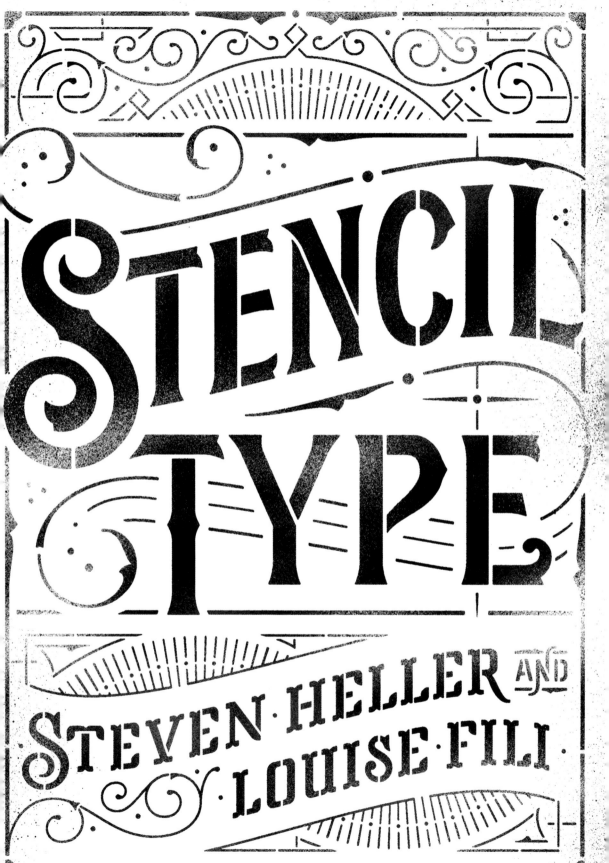

STENCIL TYPE

STEVEN HELLER AND LOUISE FILI

STEVEN HELLER is the co-chair of the MFA Design / Designer as Author + Entrepreneur program at the School of Visual Arts, New York, and the "Visuals" columnist for *The New York Times Book Review*. He is the author, editor, and co-author of over 170 books, including fifteen with Louise Fili.

LOUISE FILI is the principal of Louise Fili Ltd, a New York City-based design firm specializing in restaurant identities and food packaging. The author of *Italianissimo*, she was inducted into the Art Directors Club Hall of Fame in 2004.

Stencil Type © 2015 Steven Heller and Louise Fili

Designed by Spencer Charles/Louise Fili Ltd
Cover design by Louise Fili and Spencer Charles

First published in 2015 in hardcover in the United States of America by
Thames & Hudson Inc., 500 Fifth Avenue, New York, New York 10110

thamesandhudsonusa.com

Library of Congress Catalog Card Number 2014944626

ISBN 978-0-500-24146-2

Printed and bound in China by Everbest Printing Co Ltd

All images from the collection of Steven Heller and Louise Fili

CONTENTS

INTRODUCTION

F EW PRINTING TECHNIQUES ARE MORE PRIMITIVE THAN THE STENCIL. Early examples have been found in prehistoric caves, can be seen in ancient Chinese and Japanese art, and turn up in the arts and crafts of indigenous peoples around the world. After finger painting, stenciling—the process of spreading ink via shapes cut from paper, board, or metal—is one of the primary early learning tools for teaching children the alphabet.

Stencils are ubiquitous in the military and in the fields of industry and transportation, appearing on construction hoardings, burlap bags, foot lockers, oil drums, wine barrels, shipping containers, and more. They have a domestic function, too, when used to apply ornamental patterns to cabinets, walls, and floors, and are frequently employed—with less aesthetic fanfare—for directional and warning signs in warehouses, factories, and airports. As well as being economical and convenient in branding products and packaging or marking street signs, stencils are low-cost, mass-communication tools of populist and rebellious movements.

Stencils have at times conveyed social, political, and cultural messages. The raw improvised nature of stencil imagery and lettering implies immediacy, and demands an active response from a targeted audience. In Nazi Germany, unauthorized stenciling was used in graffiti campaigns carried out by the White Rose resistance organization; if caught, the group's members were executed. In occupied France, the stenciled letter "V" (for *victoire*) was inherently subversive and symbolically irresistible. Yet the stencil itself is a neutral facilitator—the medium is not usually the message—as evidenced by the widespread use of stencils by groups and institutions spanning all ideologies and time periods up to the present.

During the late nineteenth and early twentieth centuries, much stencil usage served a mercantile function. Artisans laboriously cut custom stencils in a number of typographic and ornamental motifs. These were often very elaborate, allowing for two or three color "masks." Such designs were an early form of branding to distinguish one maker's wares from another's, and triggered the manufacture of generic stencil apparatus, such as interlocking brass plates, which enabled users to piece together words and numbers in an efficient manner.

Stenciling was a form of typesetting that was at once movable and immovable. In the early 1900s, the firm S. G. Monce manufactured the "Improved Interchangeable 'Lock' Stencil" set with capital letters and numerals. Such kits were by necessity easy to use. The barrel-top stencil device, a slightly more advanced contraption, was a wheel with a central wooden handle and rotating brass mask that allowed the user to choose letters and numbers one at a time. It was a primitive version of early phototype machines, which used spinning wheels with type around the perimeter, and a strobe light that flashed the letters onto photo paper.

At the time, stenciling was an essential part of show-card production. The term "show card" refers to posters, advertisements, and countertop displays, custom-made for clients ranging from shop owners to carnival barkers. Tapping into the graphic styles of the day, show-card artists made everything from price tags to theater bills. Art schools offered training in show-card production, and instructional guides offered tips on how to make stencils that would last more than a few uses. Essential reading included *A Textbook on Show-Card Writing* (1903):

> "The toughest medium-weight Manila paper should be used for stencils, oiled thoroughly with boiled linseed oil, and allowed to stand at least twenty-four hours before coating both sides thinly with orange shellac. If a light quality of fiberboard is used, no preparation is necessary. A sheet of glass laid on a perfectly even table provides a surface on which the stencil can be cut with a good steel knife sharpened to a thin point. It is well to mark the ties with some bright color, to avoid cutting through them, as a single tie cut through destroys the whole stencil, and an imperfect stencil will cause more bother in its use than it is worth. It is best, therefore, never to use a patched or repaired stencil."

Making stencils is much harder than using them, and there are varying degrees of complexity. Cutting letters or images out of paper or board requires a firm grip and a good eye. The *pochoir*, a French technique distinct from ordinary stenciling, demands even more. Used extensively in the 1920s and '30s for illustrated books, book covers, and even some speciality magazines, *pochoir* is a refined method of making limited-edition stencil prints, as practiced by such visionaries as Picasso, Matisse, and Miró for their own book illustrations.

In the 1940s, Ruth Libauer Hormats, a Baltimore school teacher, invented a stencil letter-drawing system, marketed by her brother Robert Libauer, which made the creation of lettering for signs, posters, and displays much easier. The Stenso guide sheets (pp. 140–51), die-cut stencils on heavy cardboard, were state of the art for school, work, and play decades before the computer. They came in various sizes and type families, including Gothic, Old English, Frontier, Modern Script, Art Deco, and even Hebrew. Although it was a departure from the standard brass stencils once used for marking crates, Stenso was to type design what military marches are to music—functional, yet lacking in nuance. But in the same way that martial rhythms have since become absorbed into classical and popular music, so stencil lettering has influenced supposedly more sophisticated typography and graphic design.

What is it about stencils that holds sway with these "sophisticated" designers? "For me," says Jeff Levine, a designer of contemporary stencil faces, "it's the look and feel of vintage imperfection. Stencils were generally made two ways: handcut or die cut, and my designs carry both the influence of the artist (the interpretation of the letter form) and the human look of lettering made by a hands-on method (inconsistencies in stroke width, or variation of a particular letter)."

Poster and type designer Philippe Apeloig adds, "I like to use stenciled letters as heavy silhouettes, blocky type. Sometimes the letters appear almost unfinished. When the letters are stencil, they seem to be cut out of the paper. They give a kind of visual illusion, something like transparency, as if it will be possible to see through the letter shapes."

The exalted stencil in art and design, however, is not a new trend. At the turn of the last century, stencilized typefaces were introduced into magazine and poster design. These were novelty types that approximated the stencil characteristic, giving the illusion of breaks and channels between parts of letterforms. Stencils were the Modernist typographer's way of representing industry and speed, and they became recurring motifs in the art and design of the Bauhaus, De Stijl, Futurism, and Constructivism, as well as a staple of the Art Deco typographic toolkit.

In 1926, Bauhaus master Josef Albers designed *Schablonenschrift* (stencil typeface) for advertisements and large posters. "The legibility of the most commonly used typefaces decreases with distance," he wrote. "The stencil typeface increases legibility at a distance." This legibility is due to the fact that the stencil is made up of basic geometric shapes: the square; the triangle; and the quarter-circle, whose radius corresponds to the side of the square. "The unprinted portions do not remain simply blank," Albers noted, "but rather become active negatives, just as empty spaces are structured positively in architecture and sculpture."

Paul Renner, designer of the historic Futura (1927), produced an alternative, Futura Black, in 1936, which became one of the most frequently used stencil type styles from the 1930s through the 1950s. A year later, R. Hunter Middleton, for the Ludlow Typograph Company, and Gerry Powell, for American Type Founders, released similar stencil typefaces within a month of each other—both consisted only of capital letters with rounded edges and thick main strokes. With war on the not too distant horizon, usage of these de facto militarized faces had broad implications.

When Albers was experimenting with his own stencil typeface a decade earlier, he saw stencil as a means to an end. In his essay "Regarding the Economy of Typeface" (1926), he wrote, "the typographer, just like the first printers, must invent our form anew, because he most often encounters worn-out forms. To stand on his own two feet, he must reflect on the elements of layout, perhaps also study the ancients in order to recognize how they arrived at their form, and why it no longer belongs to us."

Stencils of all types are produced today. Some are new and witty, like Der Weiner Stentzel with sausage shapes for letterforms, while others, such as Bodoni or Century, are vintage faces redrawn as stencils. Along with our earlier books *Scripts* (2011) and *Shadow Type* (2013), *Stencil Type* looks at examples from the 1890s to the 1950s. There are well-known works, including Paul Rand's cigar graphics for El Producto (pp. 116–21); rare marks, such as the Spanish wine seals and labels (pp. 146–56); distinctive objects like the Montgomery Ward kitchen scale (p. 42); street signs from Venice (pp. 194–9); Métro signs from Paris (pp. 174–7); and dozens of eclectic applications of the common stencil. Common it may be, but taken en masse, a better word to describe stencil type is "extraordinary."

AMERICAN

STENCILED LETTERS ARE THE MOST POPULIST TYPOGRAPHIC STYLE in the United States. They have been, and continue to be, used prodigiously by professionals and amateurs alike to identify products and goods, make public pronouncements, and warn of imminent danger. Stencil letterforms are also closely associated with the US military, as well as the police and fire departments. Other applications of distinctly American stencil styles appear on everything from bales to boxes, fences to hoardings ("Post No Bills"), signs to banners.

In America, stenciled words and phrases are so commonplace that they are both instantly recognizable and invisible. Before the computer made typesetting accessible, children learned their ABCs in part by making words from stencils for school projects, using Ruth Libauer Hormats's Stenso Lettering Guides (pp. 140–51). Created in the 1940s, her bestselling, if functionally primitive, lettering tool offered many fashionable type styles, and was the epitome of modern, if not always the quintessence of beauty.

There was a kind of inchoate beauty in earlier stencil apparatus and the letters they produced. Most early stencils were made to be one color, but ornamental typography of the nineteenth century spawned the production of elaborate two-color stencil masks. Stencils were also inexpensive interior-decorating tools. In 1932, the Sherwin-Williams paint company, based in Cleveland, Ohio, promoted stenciled patterns for the home and office (pp. 34–5), and kits with stylish motifs encouraged homeowners to introduce personal touches.

Modern typographers, such as Paul Rand (pp. 106, 116–24), were as keen on stencil type as the more classically minded W. A. Dwiggins (pp. 72–83), who designed dozens of stencil variations. Imports from Europe, including Paul Renner's Futura Black (pp. 51–9), symbolized the Machine Age. Its angular letters and precisely carved channels dividing portions of each letterform gave the typeface its contemporary character. These channels were not simply respite for the eye, they also made the typeset words more memorable.

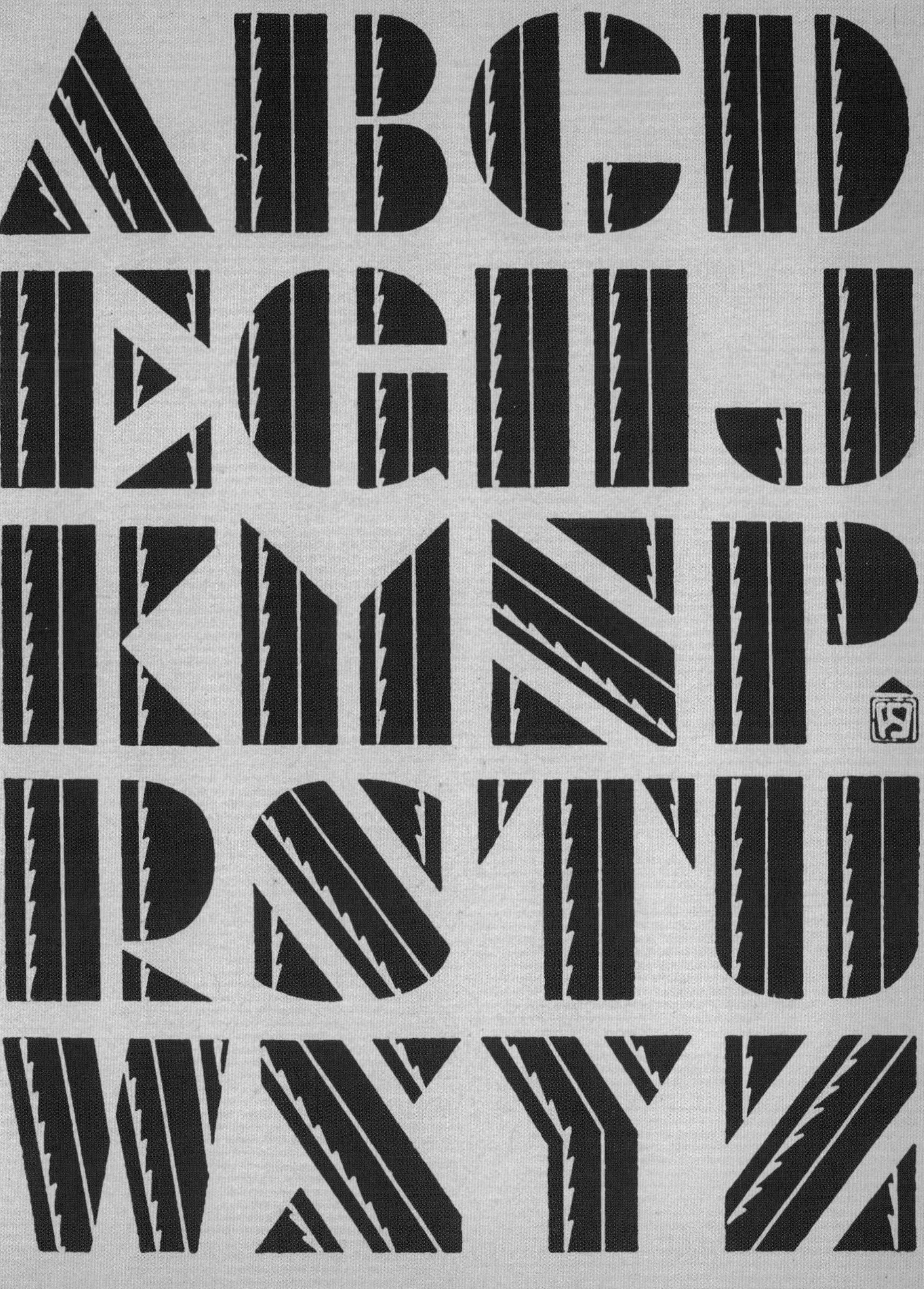

THE D.M.WY
D5

GANT CO
N.Y.
72
1
68

5

WRIGHT & WILHELMY CO.

LBS.

STANDARD BABBITT METALS

OMAHA, NEB.

10 CRANE LBS CO.

EXTRA WIPING

SOLDER

SPOKANE, WASH.

5
LBS
KOMP MACHINE WORKS
HATTIESBURG,
MISS.
5
WATKINS
MCH. & FDRY. CO.
LBS.
IMPERIAL
HATTIESBURG, MISS.

IMPORTERS OF HIGH GRADE COFFEES.

HIGH GRADE COFFEES.

19

BELL COFFEE MILLS

"TEA COFFEE

AND

CHOCOLKTES.

436 WEST 12TH St.

NEW YORK CITY.

20

LL COFFEE MILL

TEA COFFEE
AND
CHOCOLATES
36 WEST 42ND S
NEW YORK CITY

...ACE

...WICH ST.

NEW YORK.

Pan-American

MILLS.

BLACK

PEPPER

NEW YORK.

10. lbs.

POUND CAKE FLAVOR

A COMPOUND OF MACE, NUTMEG
AND CEREAL COLORED WITH
TURMERIC AND ANNATTO.
EDIBLE OIL ADDED.

FRED M. HUBER.

314 - 316 PARK AVE

BROOKLYN, N.Y.

26

lbs.   LBS.

POUND CAKE FLAVOR

FRED. W. HUBER.

314-316 PARK AVE

BROOKLYN,   N. Y.

THE

J RODONNELL CO

MACE

BEVERLEY SQUARE MARKET

GEORGE FLECK.

1222 AV. C. NEAR E. 13TH ST.

BROOKLYN, N.Y.

TEAS, COFFEES AND SPICES.

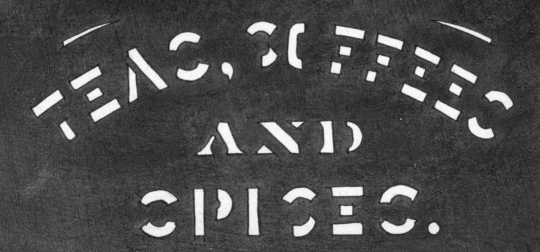

BEVERLEY SQUARE
MARKET

GEORGE MESK.

1222 A. S. NEAR E. 13TH ST.

BROOKLYN, N.Y.

TEAS, COFFEES
AND
SPICES.

BEVERAGE

STENCILS
AND
STENCIL
MATERIALS

THE SHERWIN-WILLIAMS CO.
DECORATIVE DEPARTMENT
601 CANAL ROAD
CLEVELAND, O.

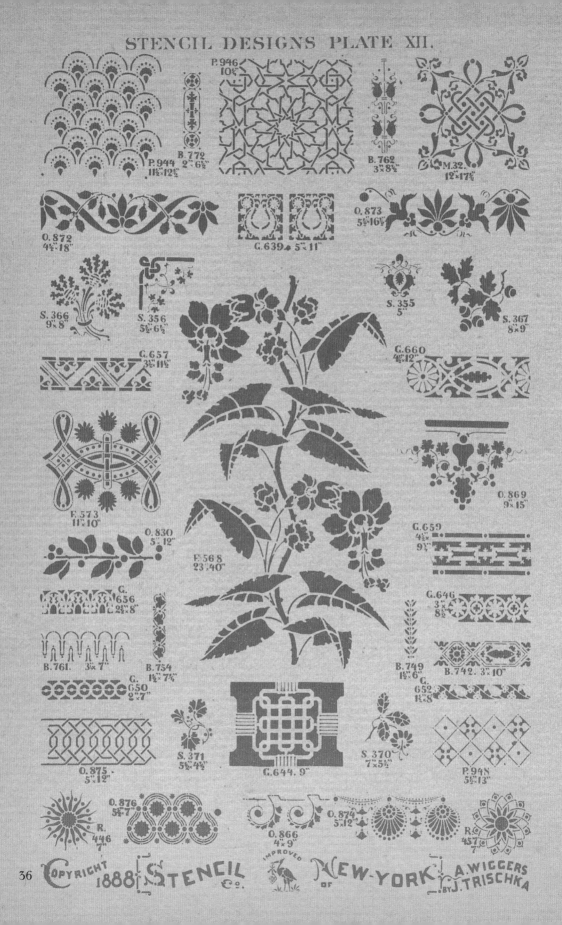

R 445 6"

C 10 2
28"-26

C 103
29"-22

S 352 7"

S 336 4½-6"   S 335 5"

S 330
2½-3½"

O 817
10"-19"

B 759
2½-7

B 757
½-7

M
23
32"

T 211
35-49½

O 839
4-13

S 346
12"-9

S 358
5"-13"

B 730 ½-5"

M 34
21"

S 350
8"

S 351
8"

F 559
7-13"

O 828
6"-10"

R 448
9"

T 232
6"-10"

G 654 1½-6"

S 329 3"-6"

T 231
12"-7"

R 450
8½"

COPYRIGHT 1888 STENCIL Co. OF NEW-YORK A. WIGGERS J. TRISCHKA IMPROVED

ALDOUS HUXLEY

POINT

COUNTER

POINT

EMPIRE STATE

ROMANCE
OF A
DICTATOR
BY GEORGE SLOCOMBE

ROMANCE
OF A
DICTATOR

BY
GEORGE
SLOCOMBE

HOUGHTON
MIFFLIN CO.

This novel is sensational news. A famous foreign correspondent takes his readers past the guards and sentries into the presence of the greatest romantic figure of the post-war age ... the modern dictator.

41

43

AMERICANA

JULY   SATIRE and HUMOR   15 cents

44

AMERICAN·PRINTER

MELLAY

AUGUST 1930 ● VOL. 91 ● NO. 2
$3 A YEAR ● 25¢ A COPY ● 9 E. 38 ST. N.Y.

MARCH 1932

VOLUME 94, NUMBER 3 · 25c A COPY, $3.00 A YEAR

EVERYDAY ART

NEWS AND COMMENT ON THE TREND
OF SCHOOL AND INDUSTRIAL ARTS

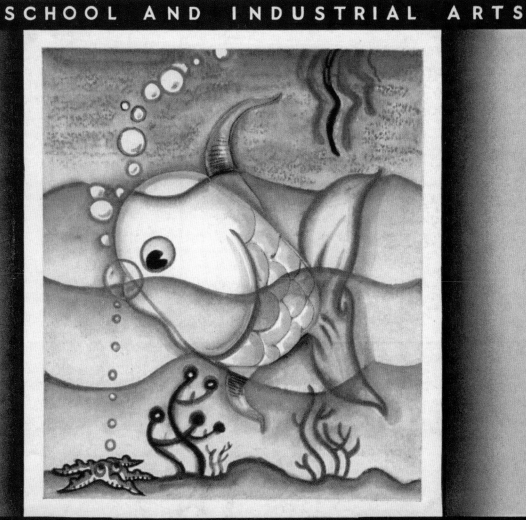

FUTURA
FUTURA
FUTURA
FUTURA
FUTURA
FUTURA
FUTURA
FUTURA
FUTURA
FUTURA
FUTURA
FUTURA
FUTURA
FUTURA
FUTURA

BAUER TYPE FOUNDRY · INC

235 EAST 45TH STREET · NEW YORK
Frankfurt am Main, Germany · Madrid and Barcelona, Spain

50

FUTURA BLACK :

GENERAL CHARACTERISTICS

In general style, Futura and Futura Black are utterly different: the former is a typographic conception of simplicity in its most abstract form; the latter, a stencil-letter, sharpened in outline and tightened in feeling... Futura Black is by no means easy to use. Unless taste and discretion are employed in good measure, it is quite likely to present a "freakish" appearance. But despite its possibilities for bizarre effects, Futura Black strikes a refreshing note in the scale of typographic "modernism." For it points to the acceptance of a principle which, more and more, is being acknowledged the backbone of real "modernism": namely, simplicity of execution combined with the adaptation and utilization of *genre*, at times *bourgeois*, sources. How often in the past decade have you noticed the original Futura Black used crudely on packing cases and subway signs! Yet this letter, glossed over as cheap and inartistic, has been refined to such an extent that it now fights for its place in the typographic sun, and with expert handling, develops a genuinely modern character.

ARTWORK etc

Any *modern* style of artwork is appropriate with Futura Black, including "loose" decorative line and wash; litho crayon; postery treatment; modern use of air brush; "free" water colors...For suitable products we suggest any ultra-modern product, service, or movement. For example, Interior Decoration in its various divisions (Furniture, Drapery, Wallpaper, Ornaments, Lighting, Accessories, etc.); Arts and Sciences, including educational courses; the newest Buildings, Hotels, Stores, etc.; Linoleum, Fabrics, Compositions, of advanced pattern or style.

BODY TYPES

20 Point 9 A 17 a

MECHANICAL ART OF PRINTING
Originality of design in showings

24 Point 8 A 15 a

POPULAR INDIAN MELODIES
For sale on Washington Street

30 Point 6 A 12 a

ADVERTISING AGENCY
With gifts unique and rare

36 Point 5 A 10 a

THE BEST READING
Woolworth Building

48 Point 5 A 9 a

AUTOMOBILES
Provincial Bank

60 Point 5 A 8 a

RESIDENCE
Music House

72/60 Point 4 A 6 a

DISPATCH
Charleston

84/72 Point 3 A 4 a

EDITION
Hamilton

TODAY AND TOMORROW

type

is part of the picture

A pronunciamento issued with profound apologies to American makers of quality paper whose concurrent statement with regard to THEIR product we have borrowed. To the great majority both statements are practically self-evident, for any graphic presentation necessitates dark on light as a medium of its perceptibility. For the artist, however, the problem lies in his attempt to establish a well-balanced relation between the two. "Divide et impera" is his device. To separate conflicting elements, to affirm governing relations, to achieve the uniformity of contrasts is the object of any artistic creation. Type, symbolic substitute of the spoken word, graphic conveyor of the message, demands the same attention in the making of an advertisement as its pictorial components. Its formative determinants observe the same constructive rules as pictorial or architectural composition. Its individuality is not based on purely technical considerations but on the manner of its presentation. The goal is to link relative elements into ONE picture of truly dramatic and arresting qualities

HUXLEY HOUSE
TYPOGRAPHERS AND DESIGNERS
117 WEST 54TH STREET • NEW YORK • CIRCLE 1792

HAIL, FUTURA BLACK!

We endorse Futura Black as a letter of display, for its decidedly modern
ectonic qualities, for its abstract and geometric design value that lends itself
o modern usage as a constructive element of the layout, as an attention-
getter and for emphasis. We also recommend its use in connection with color

55

futura
black

introducing the latest member
of the futura family, a unique
and powerful letter for display

SPEED
CHARM
VERVE

For those who demand of ships a speed that achieves the goal with the swift, true precision of a bird in flight . . . For those who indulge in the social amenities of the day and surround themselves with those elegancies that make of living a gracious art . . . For those who prefer the original of fine things rather than the duplicates . . . There are four great ships that meet every exacting requirement of speed, charm, service, cuisine . . .

MAJESTIC · OLYMPIC · HOMERIC · BELGENLAND

WHITE STAR LINE · RED STAR LINE

OFFICES IN PRINCIPAL CITIES THROUGHOUT THE WORLD · AGENCIES EVERYWHERE

FUTURA BLACK

1234567890

ABGRMNSTYZ

CDEF
IJKL
OPQR
UVWX
FRXCS

LUDLOW STENCIL

... a new typeface produced by the Ludlow Typograph Company. ... Letters with the breaks characteristic of stencils will prove useful to the typographer seeking deliberately to convey an impression of informality.

The 36 point size, title lining, is shown in the heading lines above.

36 Point Ludlow No. 41 Stencil

MITCHELL OFFERS 12
HUGE OPENING SALE

Characters in Complete Font

A B C D E F G H I J K I

M N O P Q R S T U V W

X Y Z & $ 1 2 3 4 5 6 7

8 9 0 . : , ; - ' ' ! ? — ◆

The per cent mark is sold separately

FUTURA
Black

A B C D E F G H I

J K L M N O P Q

R S T U V W X Y Z

a b c d e f g h i j

k l m n o p q r s

t u v w x y z & $

ff fi fl ft . , - : ; ! ? ')

1 2 3 4 5 6 7 8 9 0

20 Point 9A 17a

Finance Program
MODERN OFFICE

24 Point 8A 15a

Bright Moment
EXPOSITIONS

30 Point 6A 12a

Gas Age Record
BUENOS AIRES

36 Point 5A 10a

Electric Lifts
HYDRAULIC

48 Point 5A 9a

Richmond
VIRGINIA

60 Point 5A 8a

Product
FILTER

72/60 Point 4A 6a

Dealer

84/72 Point 3A 4a

Metal

REGIONAL

POSTER

EXHIBITION

NOV 18 - DEC 8

NEW YORK
AND
NEW JERSEY
FEDERAL ART PROJECT
WORKS PROGRESS
ADMINISTRATION

FEDERAL ART GALLERY
225 WEST 57th STREET NEW YORK CITY

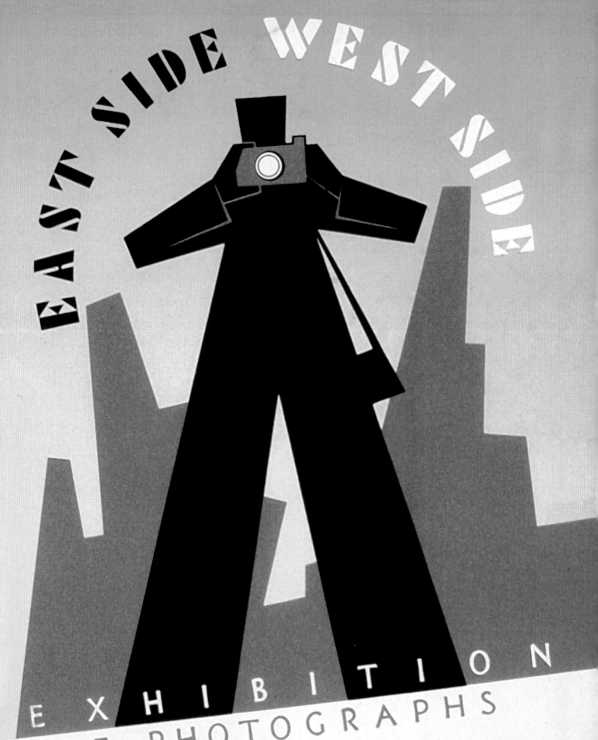

EAST SIDE WEST SIDE

EXHIBITION

OF PHOTOGRAPHS

PHOTOGRAPHY DIVISION
FEDERAL ART PROJECT
WORKS PROGRESS ADMINISTRATION
SEPTEMBER 20 THROUGH OCTOBER 4, 1938
FEDERAL ART GALLERY
225 WEST 57TH STREET
OPEN TO THE PUBLIC

63

MADE BY WPA FEDERAL ART PROJECT NYC

SING FOR YOUR SUPPER

A Topical Musical Revue

ADELPHI THEATRE
54th STREET EAST OF 7th AVE

64

HOUSEWARES

HALF-YEARLY
SALE
FIFTH FLOOR EAST BUILDING

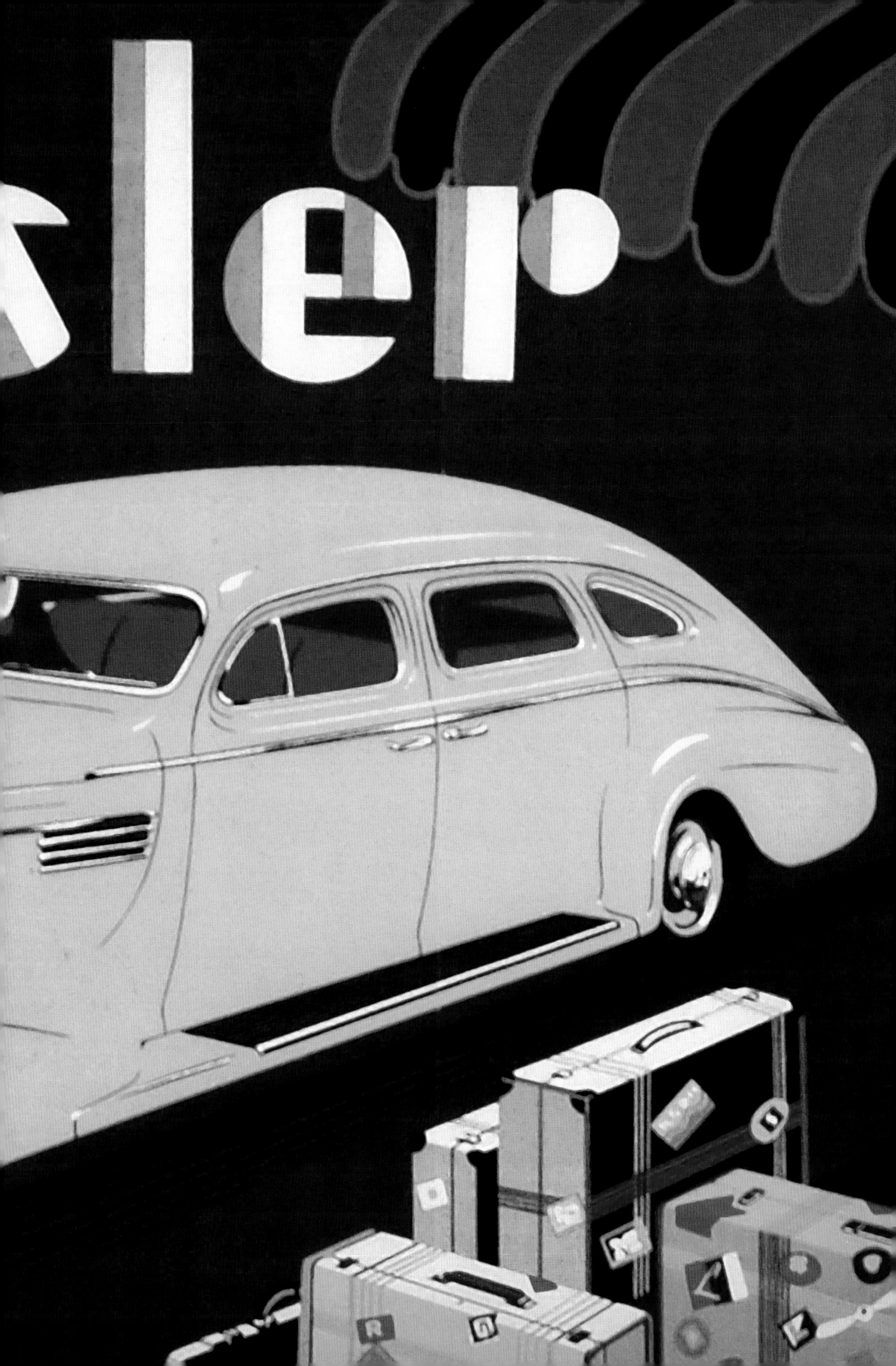
sler

JOHN DOS PASSOS

MANHATTAN TRANSFER

Salter

Simple Simon to the pie man "How do you sell your Pies?"   "I make the best by every test . . . and then I advertise."

n° 16-17

transition

synthesis

transition

n° 13

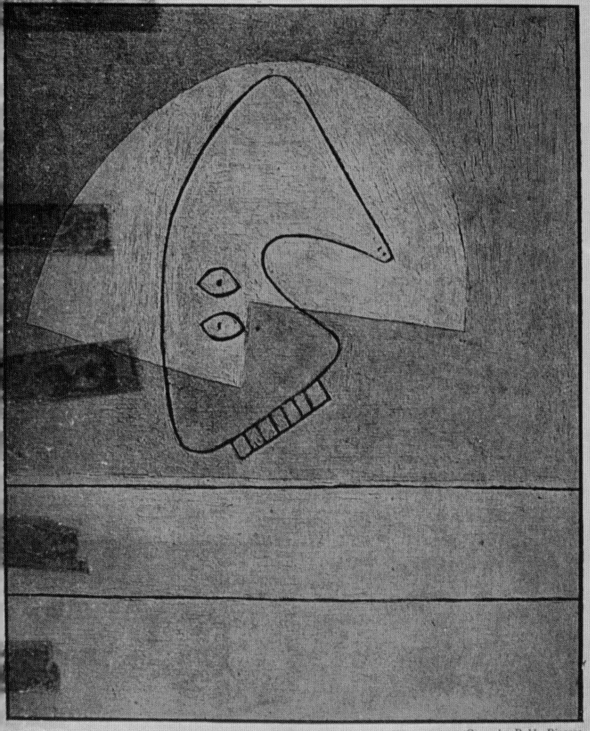

Three Designs for

SINBAD

published by

The Society of Calligraphers

1 9 2 5

Topographical Overtones

HPS

Special delivery

First class

First *class mail*

A B C D E I K M
N O P R S T U V

a b c d e f g h i j k l m
n o p q r s t u v w x y z

a c c f g i i l o r s t v y

c e g i i l
i o o r s t

Copies, N

P A   WAD

Published by

M. Firuski, Dunster House, Cambridge, Mass.

Graphic response to the stimulus CONGO

Fifty Copies, *N* WAD 57

afoil
smorst

acefgt

A B C D E F G H I J K

L M N O P R S T U V Y

ɑ ɔ c l g n o t

a b c d e f g

h i l m n p q

r s t u v

PRINTED MATTER

TO BE

Registered

 receipt requested

ABCIDEIKM

NORSUVY

einrst

ABCDEIMNORSTU

FMCSTW

AIDEMNOQRSTU

ABCD

EIMN

ORS

TUV

CAPS

lower case

alcefgik

oicstuy

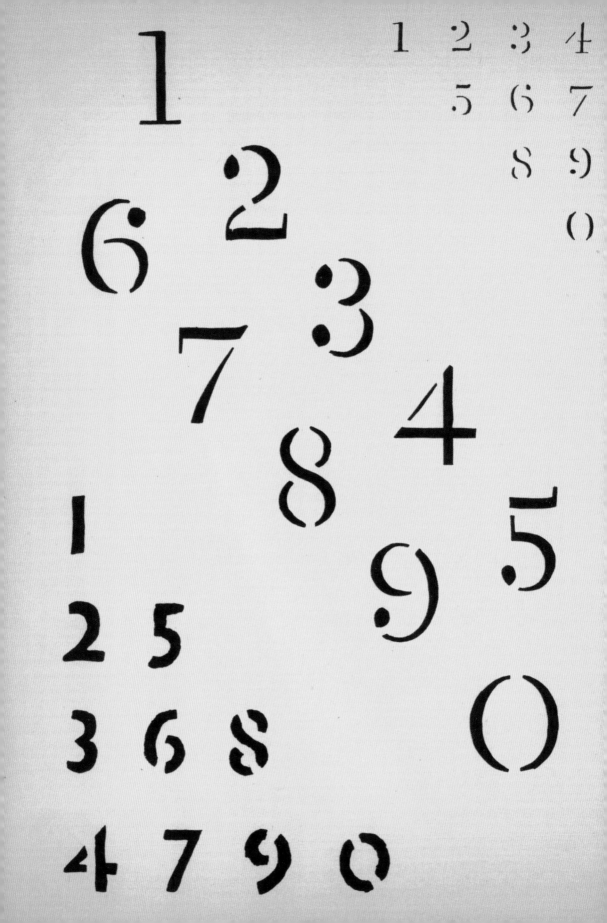

Food For T...

Hot ...

FOOD FOR THE

Hot ...

e Whole Family

hoppes

WHOLE FAMILY

Shoppes

CARGOES

June 1946

THE RAHNGHILD EDITION OF

VENUS IN FURS

BY LEOPOLD VON SACHER-MASOCH

william faro · inc

FURS

5TH AVE.

SAKS

MODERN LETTERS

POSTEI

BY· Thurlow & Hop...

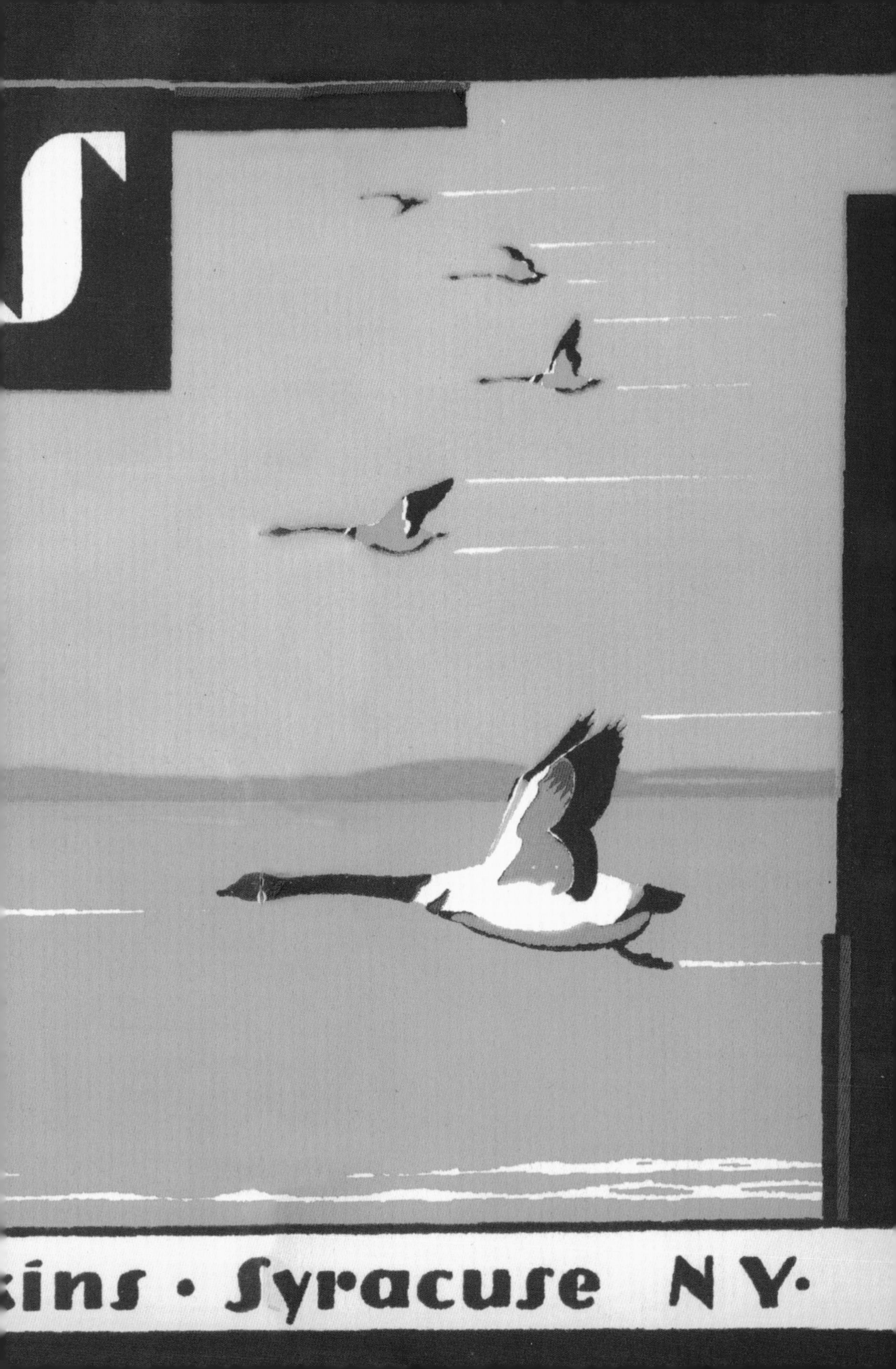
sins · Syracuse N Y ·

VI HAR BAR

THE WISE MAN ASKS FOR

GORDON'S GIN

A cocktail is no better than the gin that goes into the mixing glass. You'll learn in time that it pays to insist on genuine "Gordon's Gin"

The Heart of a good Cocktail

the theatre guild · presents
idiot's delight
by robert e sherwood

with alfred lunt lynn fontanne

alfred lunt ·
lynn fontanne

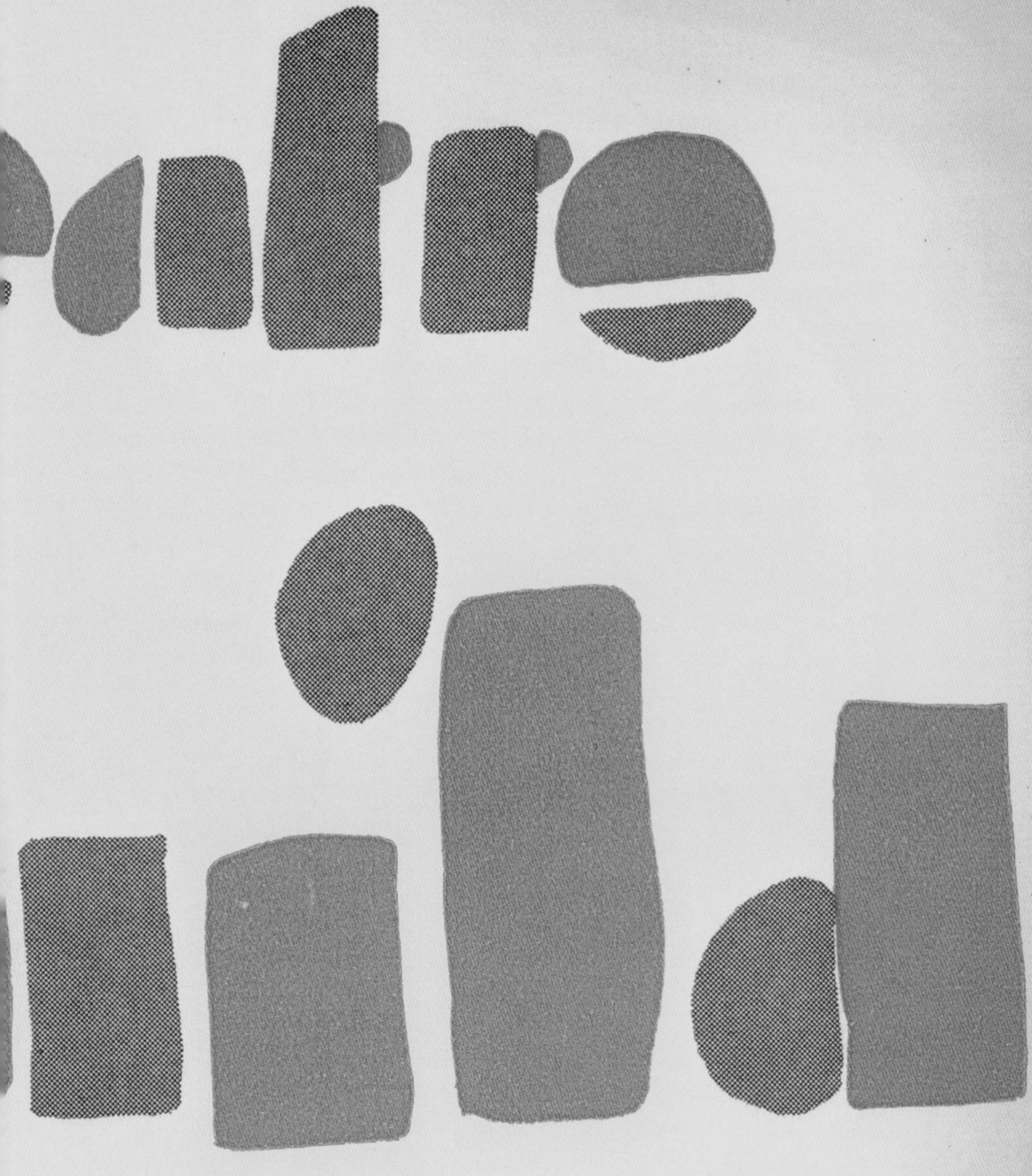

Set M = 534

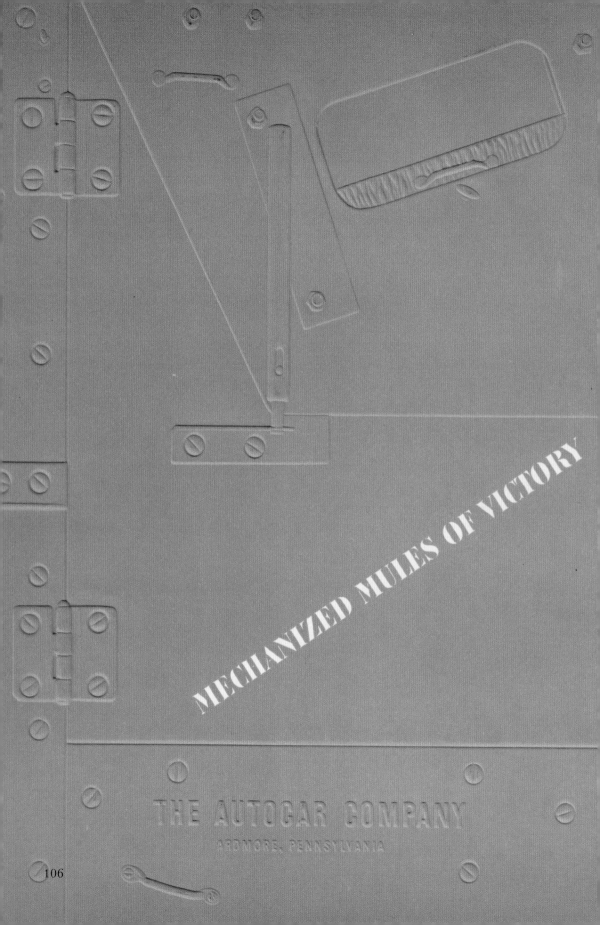

MECHANIZED MULES OF VICTORY

THE AUTOCAR COMPANY
ARDMORE, PENNSYLVANIA

CREATIVE CHEMISTRY

EDWIN E. SLOSSON

"Quality Tells"

STENCIL

BY **AMERICAN** TYPE FOUNDERS •

THE ROLLER BEARING CORPORATION

RBC

101 TRENTON AVENUE
NEWARK, NEW JERSEY

STATE
S.S.
LINES

END OF THE
MONTH
SALE
AT LACY'S

MODERN

60 POINT 3A $8.50

MODERN TYPO

36 POINT 5A $5.00

MODERN TYPOGRAPH

24 POINT 7A $3.20

0 1 2 3 4 5 6 7 8 9 10 11 12 13 14 15 16 17 18 19 20 21 22 23 24 25 26 27 28

ABCDEFGHIJKLMNOPQRST

MODERN T

48 POINT   3A $6.40

MODERN TYPOGR

30 POINT   6A $4.40

MODERN TYPOGRAPHY IS FO

18 POINT   10A $2.75

0 1 2 3 4 5 6 7 8 9 10 11 12 13 14 15 16 17 18 19 20 21 22 23 24 25 26 27 28

WXYZ&$1234567890¢.,-'';;!?

113

ALPHA BLOX

- Made in ◢ linear and ◤ reverse—cut and cast to register for two-color work ◢ Both these styles are available in 12, 24, and 36 pt. sizes

→ Ꭺ Ꭺ Ꭺ

→ a a a

◢ LPHA-BLOX save the cost of artwork and engravings. Use them as ornaments, backgrounds, initials, complete words, and in border designs

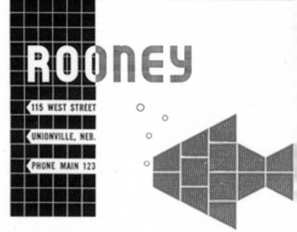

◼ RINTING is a vital contribution among the arts of man. In its higher employment it helps interpret truths of divine import. Through printing, we may confer with all the noble spirits of preceding ages and delve into the wealth of knowledge acquired by men from the dawn of writing. This is a truth of surpassing import. Fully comprehended it opens to a printer a broad field of usefulness which few other crafts can rival.

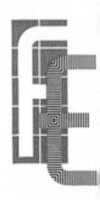

CHARACTERS IN COMPLETE FONTS

LINEAR

CHARACTER NO.	1	2	3	4	5	6	7	8	9	10	11	12	13	14	15	16	17	18	19
QUANTITY IN FONT 12 PT.	90	22	50	40	20	100	10	16	14	10	10	10	10	10	10	16	10	10	
24 PT.	44	14	30	24	12	56	6	12	10	6	6	6	6	6	6	8	6	6	
36 PT.	32	10	24	16	8	40	4	10	8	4	4	4	4	4	4	8	4	4	

Prices: 12 pt.... 3.90 — 24 pt.... 7.80 — 36 pt.... 11.70

REVERSE

CHARACTER NO.	21	22	23	24	25	26	27	28	29	210	211	212	213	214	215	216	217	218	219	220	221	222	223
QUANTITY IN FONT 12 PT.	100	20	46	36	18	120	10	18	16	10	10	12	10	10	10	10	10	10	60	20	20	20	
24 PT.	44	14	30	24	12	56	6	12	10	6	6	6	6	6	6	6	6	42	8	8	8		
36 PT.	32	8	24	16	8	40	4	10	8	4	4	4	4	4	4	4	36	8	8	8			

Prices: 12 pt.... 4.80 — 24 pt.... 9.35 — 36 pt.... 14.60

ABCDE
FGHIJK
LMNOP
QRSTU
VWXYZ
1234567890

EL PRO

EL PRO

for a
brighter
Christmas

ODUCTO

Paul Rand

EL PRO

DUCTO

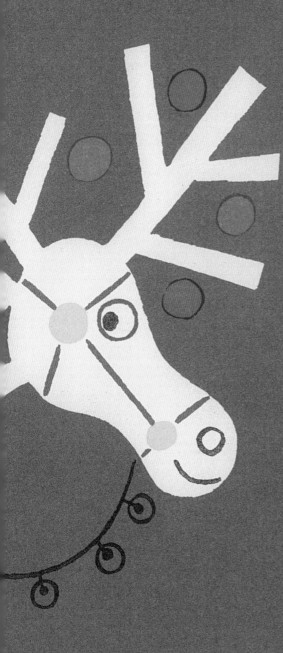

Paul Rand

DIRECTION

April-May 1941 vol 4 # 4 15¢

DIRECTION

Vol 5 # 2

April - May 1942

15¢

Kaiser

for 1951

Built to better the best on the road

PRESTIGE IN PAPER

MULTIPLIES RESULTS . . . . IN-
CREASES THE RESPONSES TO
DIRECT BY MAIL ADVERTISING
BY INSPIRING INTEREST AT THE
FIRST GLANCE. IMPORTANT
BOOKLETS. ANNOUNCEMENTS.
DEMAND AN IMPORTANT EN-
VELOPE PAPER . . . . TO PROTECT
THE CONTENTS . . . . TO GAIN AN
AUDIENCE. TO CONVEY PRESTIGE.
A MITSCHERLICH ENVELOPE PA-
PER ASSURES FINE APPEAR-
ANCE. IT MAKES A HANDSOMER.
MORE LASTING ENVELOPE . . . .
CORNERS SQUARE. UNBENT . . . .
EDGES SHARP. UNFRAYED. IT'S
STRONG. CLEAN AND MADE TO
SPECIFICATION - - - A PERFECT
PAPER FOR THIS PURPOSE.

PORT HURON
SULPHITE AND PAPER COMPANY

NEW YORK   PORT HURON. MICH.   CHICAGO

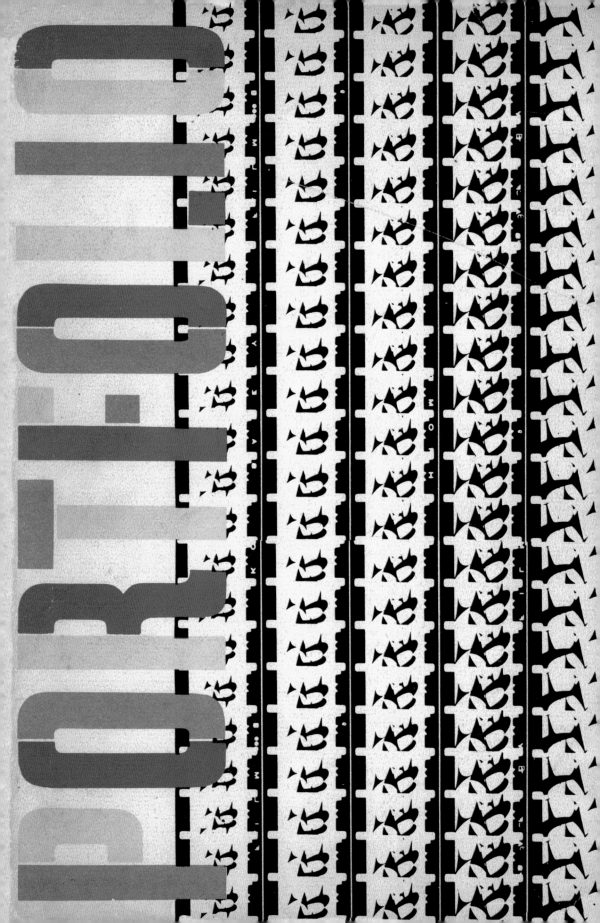

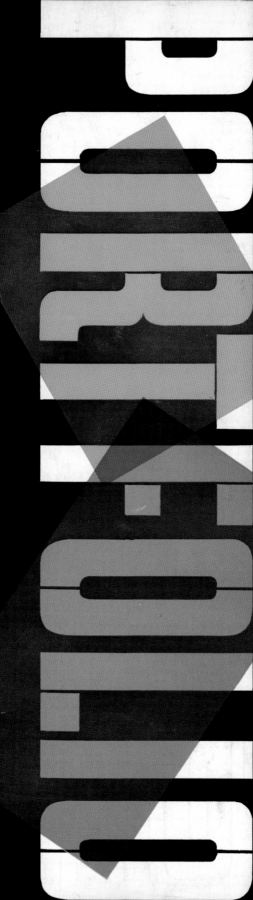

AMERICA AT WAR

Series of 1942

138

West Virginia Pulp and Paper Company

"America at War" by Anton Otto Fischer

WESTVACO Inspirations for Printers 138

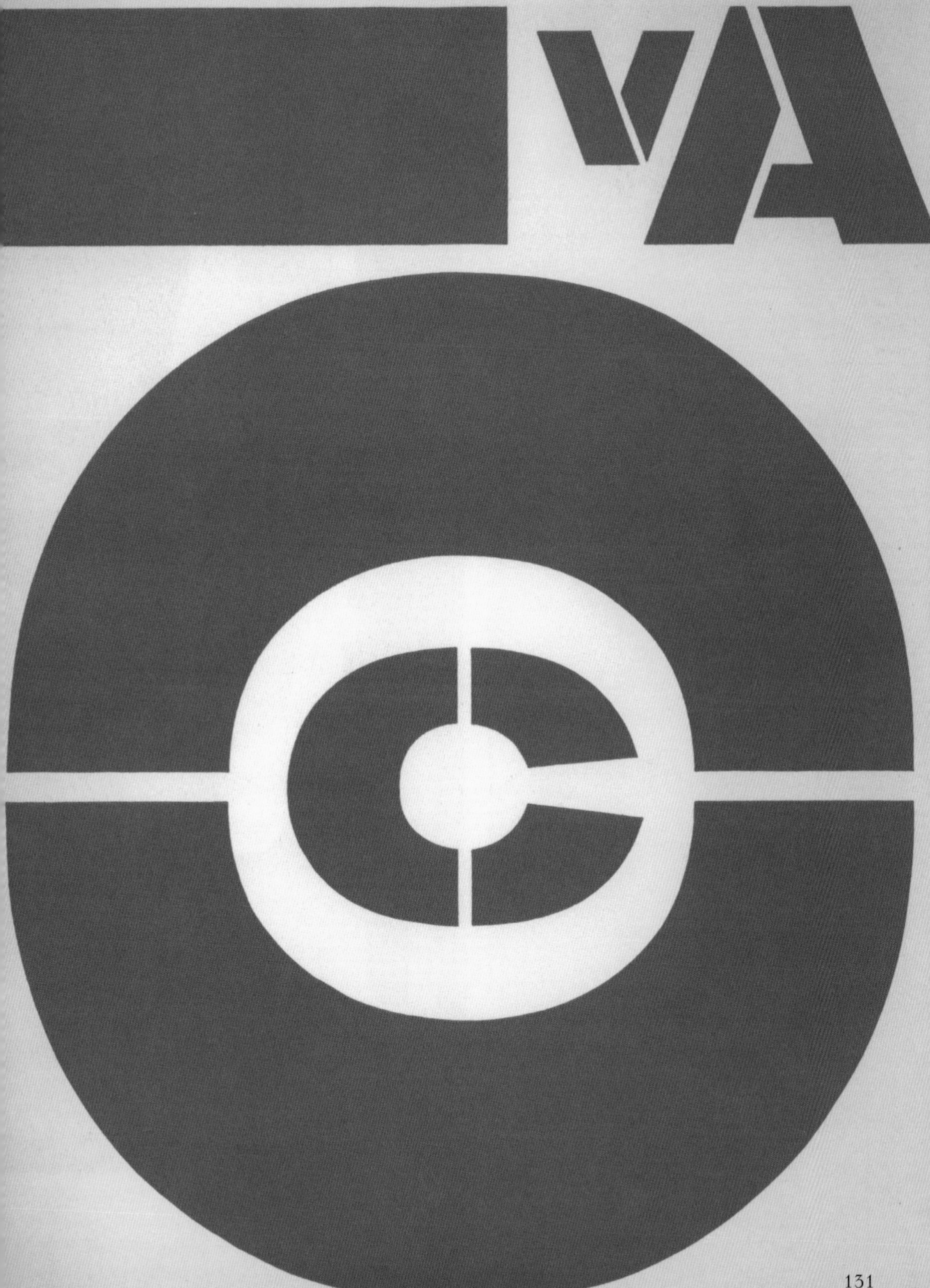
vA

The CRADLE of the DEEP

"Whether it be regarded as an account of actual experience or as a piece of imaginative writing, it is a book of unusual quality."
ST. JOHN ERVINE

"Invention or no, The Cradle of the Deep is a work of the most lively entertainment."
HUGH WALPOLE

by JOAN LOWELL

ENCOUNTER with REVOLUTION

Understanding the
social upheaval
that surrounds us...
and the positive
role it demands of
Americans today

M. RICHARD SHAULL

EGYPT

PARIS

KHIVA

BERLIN

LUXOR

EUROPA ABCDE

ABCDEFGHIKLMNOPQRSTUVWXYZ

PASCOE

a special offer

HO CHI MINH

PRISON DIARY

HANOI – 1978

STENSO LETTERING SET No. 45

A B C D E
(ACTUAL SIZE OF LETTERS)

a b c d e f g

1¼" GOTHIC LETTERS

A B C D E
F G H I J K
L M N O
Q R S T
V W X Y Z
. , : ; ? ! -

1¼" GOTHIC LETTERS & NUMBERS

a b c d e f g
h i j k l m n
q r s t u
v w x y z 0
1 2 3 4 5
6 7 8 9 !

SET OF 2 GUIDES

STENSO LETTERING GUIDES
are made from Treated Stencil Board
- ✓ EASY TO USE
- ✓ DURABLE
- ✓ PRECISELY ACCURATE

30¢

STENSO LETTERING CO.,   Industrial Bldg.,   Baltimore 2, Md.   MADE IN U.S.

TRADE
STENSO
MARK
Reg U S Pat Off

STENSO LETTERING SET No. 44

ABCDEF

(ACTUAL SIZE OF LETTERS)

GHIJKL

1-INCH ROMAN LETTERS

BCDEF
GHIJKL
MNOPQ
RSTUV
WXYZ&

1-INCH NUMBERS & DESIGNS

123456
7890$¢
;!?-+÷

SET OF 2 GUIDES

STENSO LETTERING CO.

STENSO LETTERING GUIDES

30¢

are made from Treated Stencil Board
✓ **EASY TO USE**   ✓ **DURABLE**
✓ **PRECISELY ACCURATE**

ENSO LETTERING CO.,   Industrial Bldg.,   Baltimore 2, Md.   MADE IN U.S.A.

TRADE
STENSO
MARK
Reg. U. S. Pat. Of.

STENSO

½ Inch ROMAN LETTERS AND NUMBERS

STENSO LETTERING GUIDE No. 12, ½ Inch Roman

ABCDEFGHI
JKLMNOPQ
RSTUVWXY
Z&?!¡:1234
567890$¢

REG. U. S. PAT. OFF.   BALTIMORE 18, MARYLAND
MADE IN U. S. A.
STENSO LETTERING CO.

TRADE STENSO MARK
REG. U. S. PAT. OFF.

© 1956 STENSO LETTERING CO. 1101 E. 25th ST., BALTIMORE 18, MD. MADE IN U. S. A.

INEXPENSIVE DURABLE EASY TO USE

Perfect Lettering is Easy with

15¢

Stenso® Let

Inch Modern Script Letters and Numbers
PAT. PENDING

NO

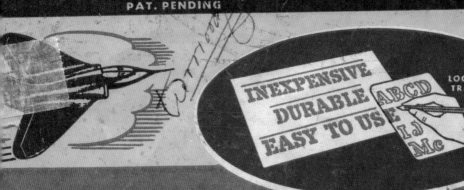

INEXPENSIVE
DURABLE
EASY TO USE

LOOK FOR THIS TRADE MARK

ABCD
IJ
Mc

STENSO LETTERING GUIDE No. 51 · ¾ Inch Modern Script
PAT. PENDING

A B C D E F G H I J K
L M N O P Q R S T U
V W X Y Z & $ ¢

1 CARD—¾" SIZE

1 2 3 4 5 6 7 8 9 0 b

a b c d e f g h i j k l m n o
p q r s t u v w x y z

1101 EAST 25th STREET
BALTIMORE 18, MARYLAND
MADE IN U.S.A.

143

EASY TO USE FOR PERFECT LETTERING

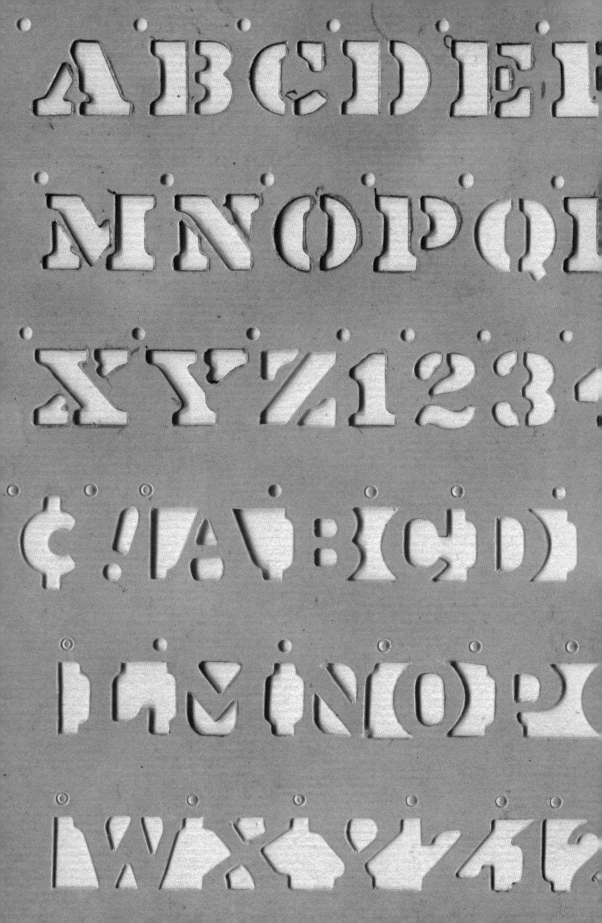

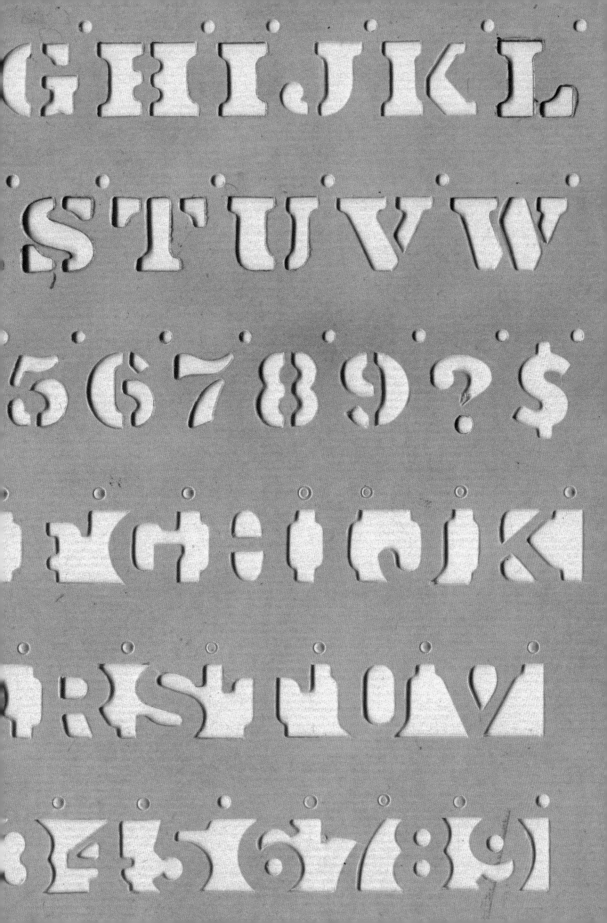

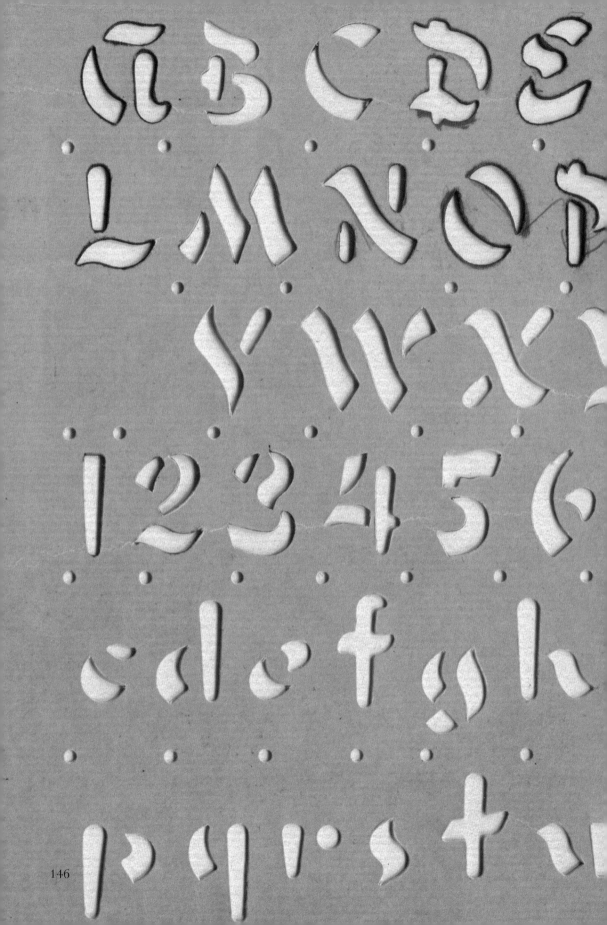

146

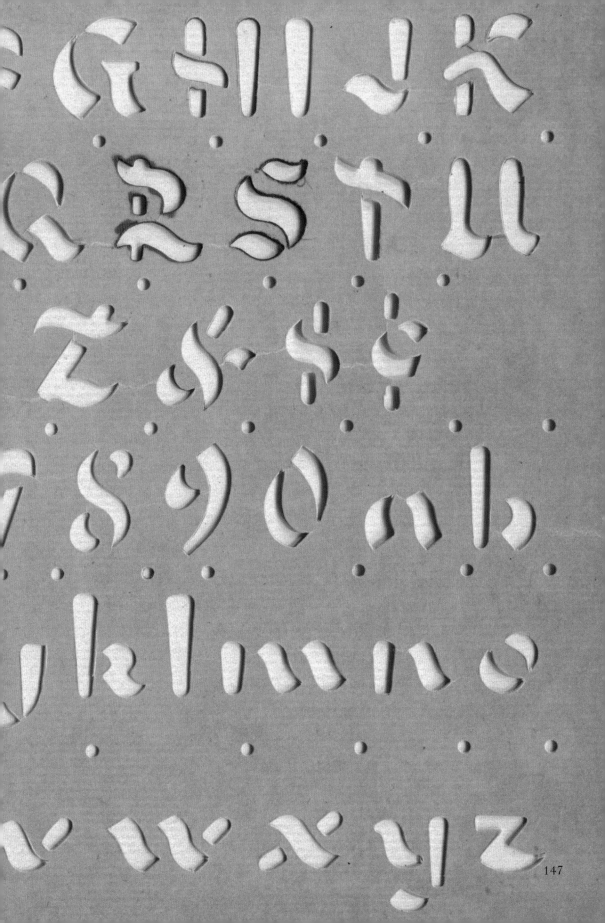

ABCDEF
GHIJKL
MNOPQ
RSTUV
WXYZ&

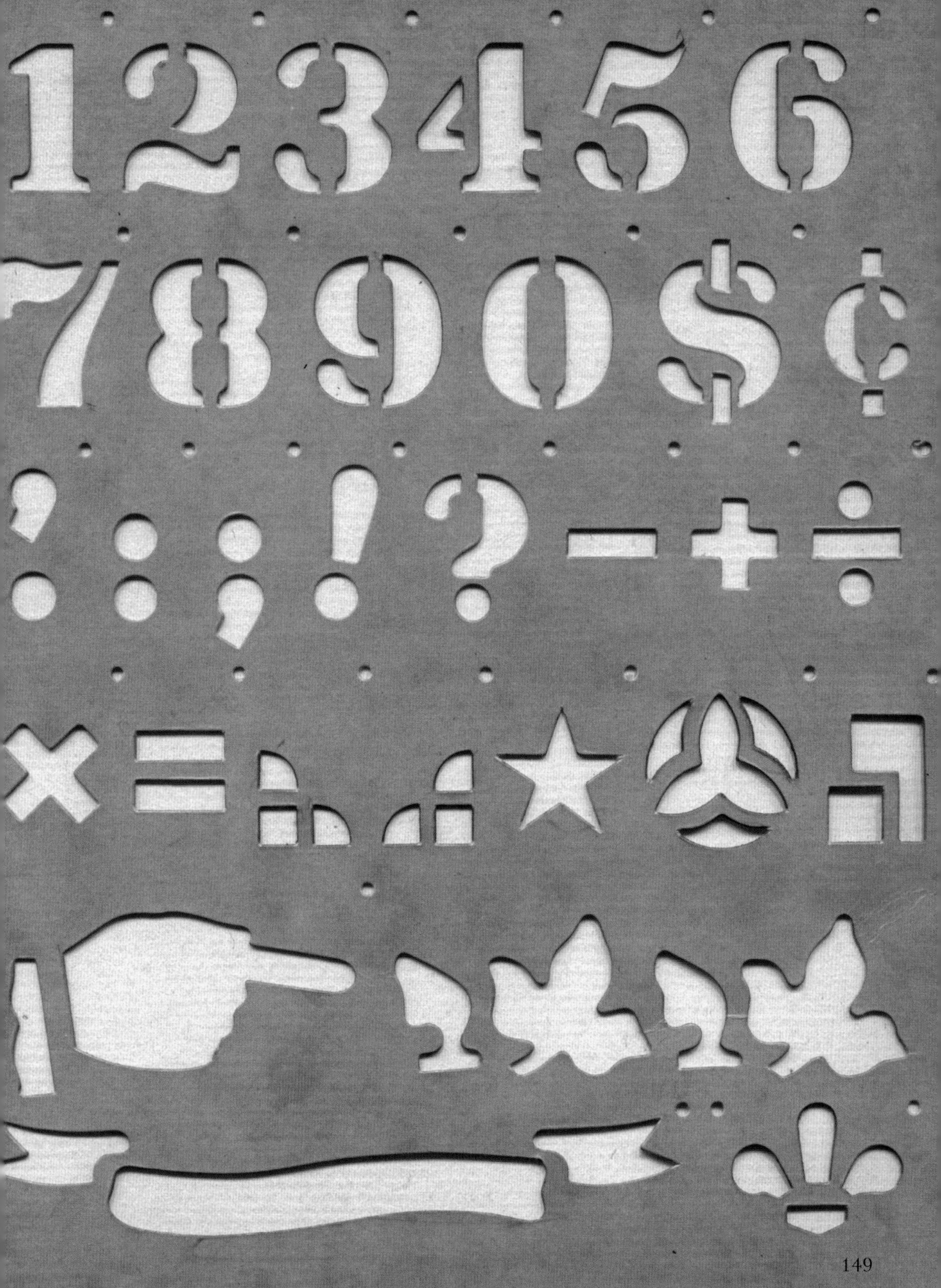
123456
7890$¢
,:;!?−+÷
×=

ABCDE
FGHIJK
LMNOP
QRSTU
VWXYZ
&$¢?!;

abcdefg
hijklmn
opqrstu
vwxyz0
12345
6789!

151

WLS FAMILY ALBUM 1934

10th Anniversary

11. Stencil influenced alphabet from *Practical Lettering: Modern and Foreign* by Samuel Welo, Frederick J. Drake & Co., Chicago, 1930.

12–17. Metallic stencil masks, *c.* 1900–10.

18–20. Oak tag handcut stencils for various businesses, *c.* 1895.

21. Sketch for oak tag stencil, *c.* 1895.

22–31. Oak tag handcut stencils for various businesses, *c.* 1895.

32–3. Handpainted stencil on Orange Crush box, 1948.

34–7. Book cover and pages from *Stencils and Stencil Materials*, Sherwin-Williams, Cleveland, Ohio, 1932.

38. Book jacket for *Point Counter Point*, designed by E. McKnight Kauffer, Modern Library, New York, 1928.

39. Cover for Empire State Building souvenir catalog, 1932.

40. Tin for Penthouse Chocolate Tid Bits, *c.* 1930.

41. Book jacket for *Romance of a Dictator*, Houghton Mifflin Co., Boston, 1932.

42. Kitchen scale, Montgomery Ward, *c.* 1935.

43. Electric wall clock, Telechron, *c.* 1948.

44. Magazine cover for *Americana, Satire and Humor*, New York, July 1932.

45. Magazine cover for *American Printer*, designed by Metlav, August 1930.

46. Magazine cover for *American Printer*, March 1932.

47. Magazine cover for *Everyday Art*, Sandusky, Ohio, and New York, 1937.

48. Magazine cover for *PM*, designed by Joseph Binder, New York, April–May 1940.

49. Magazine cover for *What's New*, *c.* 1933.

50. Futura type specimen, designed by Paul Renner, Bauer Type Foundry, New York, 1936.

51. Futura Black type specimen, designed by Paul Renner, Bauer Type Foundry, New York, 1936.

52–7 Futura Black type specimen, designed by Paul Renner, Huxley House, New York, 1937.

58–9 Futura Black type specimen, from untitled specimen portfolio, *c.* 1936.

60. Ludlow Stencil type specimen, designed by R. Hunter Middleton, Ludlow Typograph Company, Chicago, 1938.

61. Futura Black type specimen, designed by Paul Renner, Bauer Type Foundry, New York, 1936.

62. Poster for the *Regional Poster Exhibition*, Federal Art Gallery, New York, *c.* 1938.

63. Poster for *East Side West Side Exhibition of Photographs*, Federal Art Gallery, New York, 1938.

64. Poster for *Sing For Your Supper*, Adelphi Theatre, New York, 1938.

65. Poster for housewares half-yearly sale, Macy's department store, New York, 1936.

66–7. Billboard design for Chrysler Corporation, Detroit, *c.* 1938.

68. Book jacket for *Manhattan Transfer*, designed by George Salter, Somerset Books, New York, 1925.

69. Magazine cover for *More Business*, April 1933.

70. Magazine cover for *Transition*, designed by Paval, 1929.

71. Magazine cover for *Transition*, by Picasso, 1928.

72–83. Stencils by W. A. Dwiggins, from *Stenciled Ornament and Illustration: A Demonstration of William Addison Dwiggins' Method of Book Decoration and Other Uses of the Stencil* by Dorothy Abbe, Puterschein-Hingham, Hingham, Massachusetts, 1979.

84–5. Billboards for Hot Shoppes, from *Modern Sign Painting* by Edward J. Duvall, Frederick J. Drake & Co., Chicago, 1949.

86–7. Window signs for The Esther Shop, from *Modern Sign Painting* by Edward J. Duvall, Frederick J. Drake & Co., Chicago, 1949.

88. Magazine cover for *Cargoes*, Abraham Lincoln High School, Brooklyn, New York (Leon Friend, instructor), June 1946.

89. Title page from *Venus in Furs*, William Faro, New York, 1932.

90. "83," designer and date unknown.

91. Magazine cover for *Broom*, designed by Fernand Léger, 1922.

92. "Furs," for Saks Fifth Avenue, New York, from untitled sketchbook, 1934.

93. "Modern Letters," from untitled sketchbook, 1934.

94–5. Advertising poster from untitled sketchbook, *c.* 1935.

96. "VI HAR BAR," from untitled sketchbook, *c.* 1935.

97. Magazine advertisement for Gordon's Gin, 1946.

98–101. Program cover for *Idiot's Delight*, The Theatre Guild, New York, 1936.

102–3. Record cover for *Songs of Free Men*, designed by Alex Steinweiss, New York, 1942.

104. Paper sample booklet for Coty, designed by J. R. McKinney, *c.* 1930.

105. Book jacket for *Art Now*, designed by E. McKnight Kauffer, Faber & Faber, London, 1933.

106. Catalog cover for *Mechanized Mules of Victory*, designed by Paul Rand, The AutoCar Company, Ardmore, Pennsylvania, 1941.

107. Book jacket for *Creative Chemistry*, designed by "CL," *c.* 1938.

108–9. Storefront design for Radio Shop, *c.* 1946.

110. Advertisement for Vat 69 whisky, 1943.

111–13. Stencil type specimen by American Type Founders, Elizabeth, New Jersey, 1950.

114. Alpha Blox type specimen by American Type Founders, Elizabeth, New Jersey, 1944.

115. Stencil capital letters and numerals by W. Ben Hunt and Edward C. Hunt, 1937.

116–17. Logo and cigar gift box for El Producto, Philadelphia, Pennsylvania, designed by Paul Rand, 1952.

118–21. Advertisements for El Producto, Philadelphia, Pennsylvania, designed by Paul Rand, 1953–7.

122. Magazine cover for *Direction*, designed by Paul Rand, April–May 1941.

123. Magazine cover for *Direction*, designed by Paul Rand, April–May 1942.

124. Brochure for Kaiser Motors, Willow Run, Michigan, designed by Paul Rand, 1951.

125. Advertisement for Port Huron Sulphite & Paper Co., Michigan, 1939.

126. Magazine cover for *Portfolio No. 3*, designed by Alexey Brodovitch, Winter 1951.

127. Magazine cover for *Portfolio No. 1*, designed by Alexey Brodovitch, Winter 1950.

128–9. Title page for *Westvaco Inspirations for Printers 138*, designed by Bradbury Thompson, 1942.

129. Magazine cover for *Westvaco Inspirations for Printers 138*, designed by Bradbury Thompson, 1942.

130–1. Inside cover for *Westvaco Inspirations for Printers 138*, designed by Bradbury Thompson, 1942.

132. "Wet Paint" sign for Touraine Paints, Everett, Massachusetts, *c.* 1950s.

133. Book jacket for *The Cradle of the Deep*, Simon & Schuster, New York, 1929.

134. Book jacket for *Encounter with Revolution*, Association Press, New York, 1952.

135. Europa type specimen, handlettered variation of Future Black, *c.* 1937.

136. Catalog cover for Pascoe Industries, New York, 1949.

137. Book jacket for *Prison Diary*, Foreign Language Press, Hanoi, 1978.

138–9. Inside cover for *Westvaco Inspirations for Printers 200*, designed by Bradbury Thompson, 1955.

140–51. Stenso Lettering Set package and templates, 1955–8.

152. Radio program cover for *WLS Family Album*, Prairie Farmer Publishing Co., Chicago, 1934.

FRENCH

T HE FRENCH HAVE A CELEBRATED HISTORY OF STENCILED ART
and design. The most recognized process is *pochoir*, which reached its zenith
in the early twentieth century. A more refined printing method than quotidian
stencils, *pochoir* is known, as Stephen H. Van Dyk and Carolyn Siegel, curators
of *Vibrant Visions: Pochoir Prints in the Cooper-Hewitt National Design Museum
Library*, wrote in the exhibition catalog, for "crisp lines and brilliant colors" and
for producing "images that have a freshly printed or wet appearance."

The method was used to create prints for fashion, patterns, and architectural
design, and is often linked to Art Nouveau and Art Deco book illustration. The
quintessence of stencil image-making, *pochoir* is rarely used as a lettering tool.
An even more poetic, if old-fashioned, term for stenciled alphabets is *lettres à jour*,
which type historian James Mosley defined in an essay for St. Bride Library in
London as "letters through which you see daylight." He added that, "sometimes
they are quite elegantly set out and occasionally they are chaotic, but the letters
themselves are beautifully drawn and the notices always have a living quality."

As early as the eighteenth century, stencil templates were available for sale in a
limited assortment of styles. A century later, the basic stencil alphabet was derived
from Didot (pp. 164–5), and sold either as individual letters or custom-cut for
industrial and mercantile applications. The stencil is an essential element in the
graphic language of Parisian streets. Many of the older Métro station signs have
stencil characteristics as part or all their letters (pp. 174–5), and shop signs and
other vintage "street jewelry," such as gas-pipe caps and sewer covers, are stamped
with stenciled types, which were decidedly functional and low cost.

As a weapon in the aesthetic revolution against traditional art, the stencil cap-
tured the fascination of many modern French artists, who combined the sculptural aspect of typefaces and the freehand virtue of stencil to make expressive art.
Rendering everyday type by hand released the artist from the confining rules of
typography, and enabled the creation of new and experimental letters that could
be legible or illegible, recognizable or novel.

A B C D E

F G H I J

K L M N O

P Q R S T

U V X Y Z

BILL
DO
BELL
LET

ETS

S

&

TRES

4 A   24 POINT

PROCTOR & GAMBLE
1234567890

4 A   36 POINT

WANAMAKER

3 A   48 POINT

REVILLON

3 A   60 POINT

HARPERS

DELACROIX

EDISON

LA FONTAINE

BERLIOZ - RICHELIEU - PASCAL

NAPOLÉON

TURENNE

PARMENTIER

les robes
de vos rô
ves selon
l'issues en

SÉTILOSE

CAFÉ EXTRA

125 gr.   Net

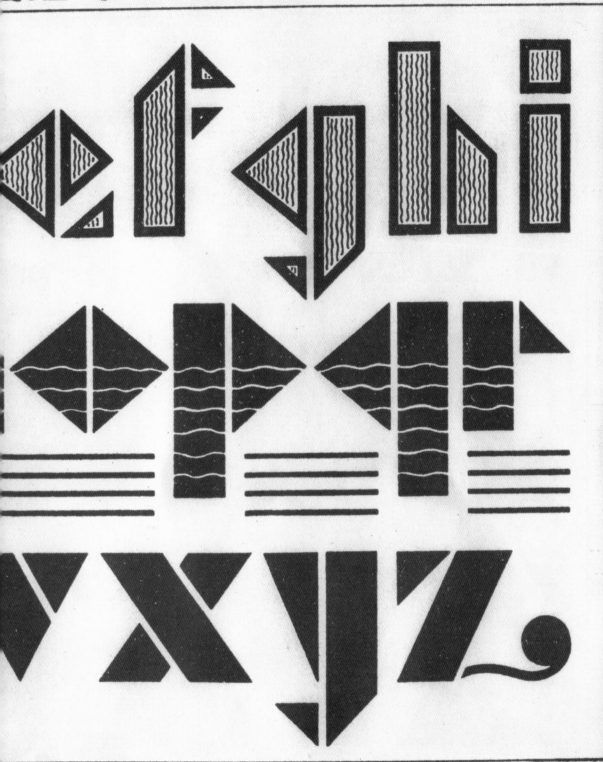

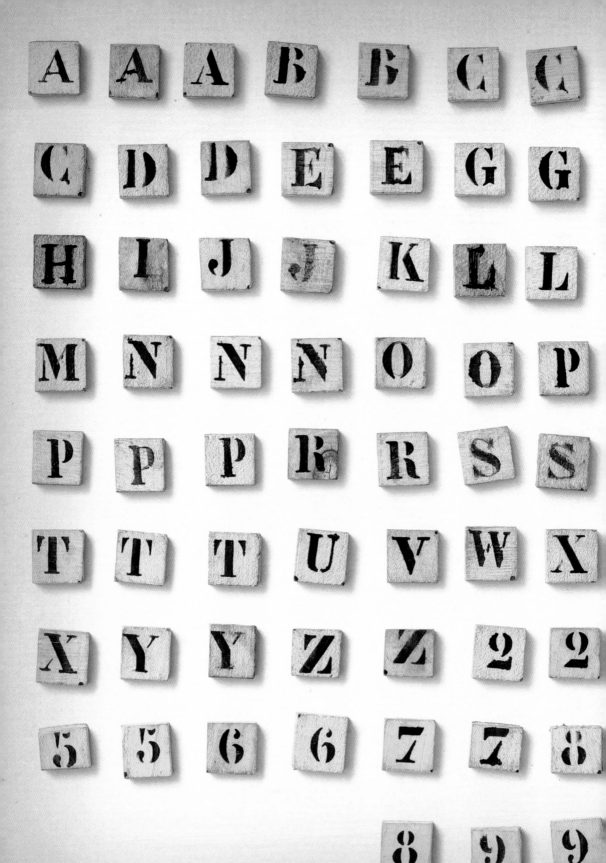

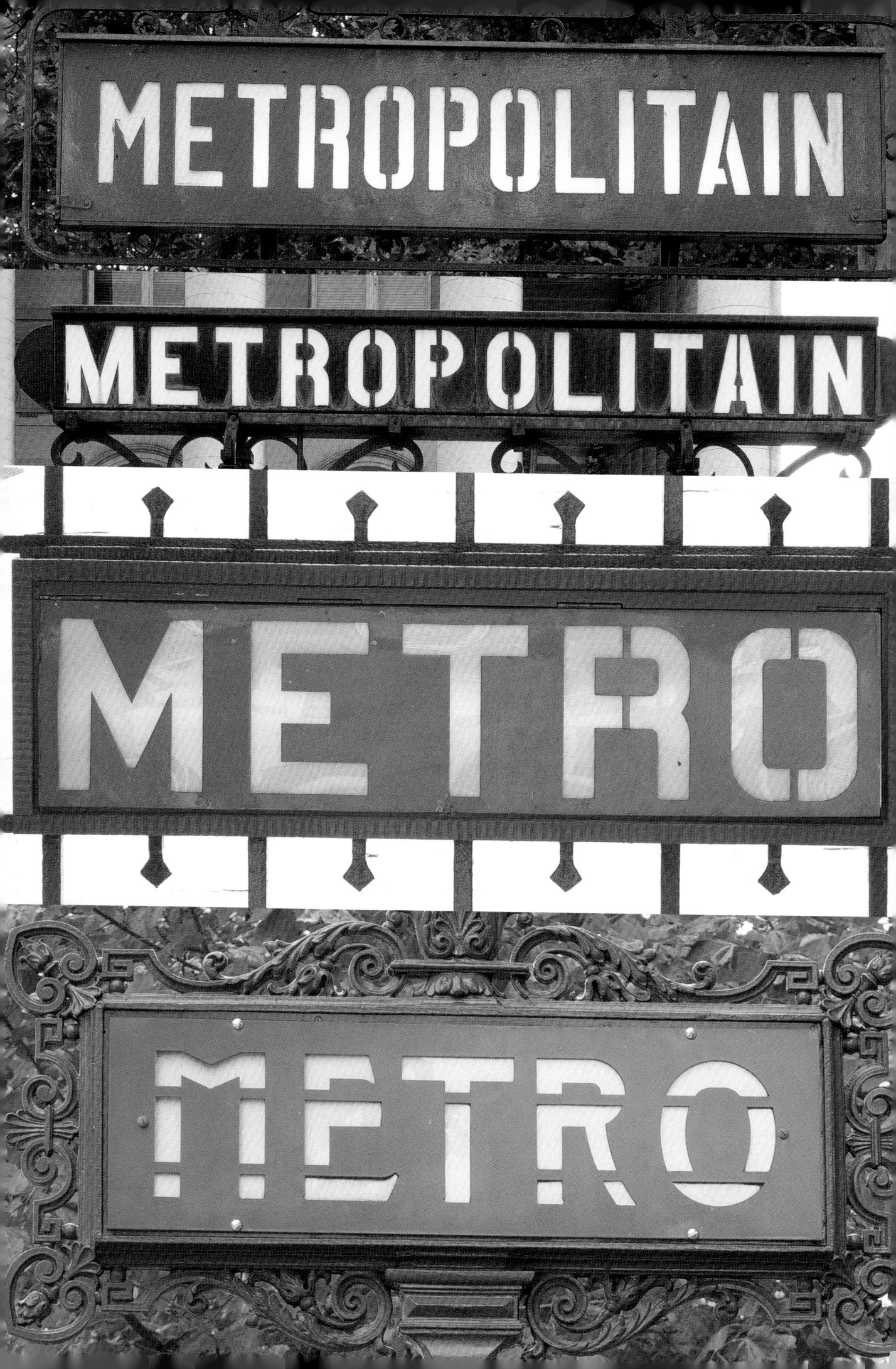
METROPOLITAIN
METROPOLITAIN
METRO
METRO

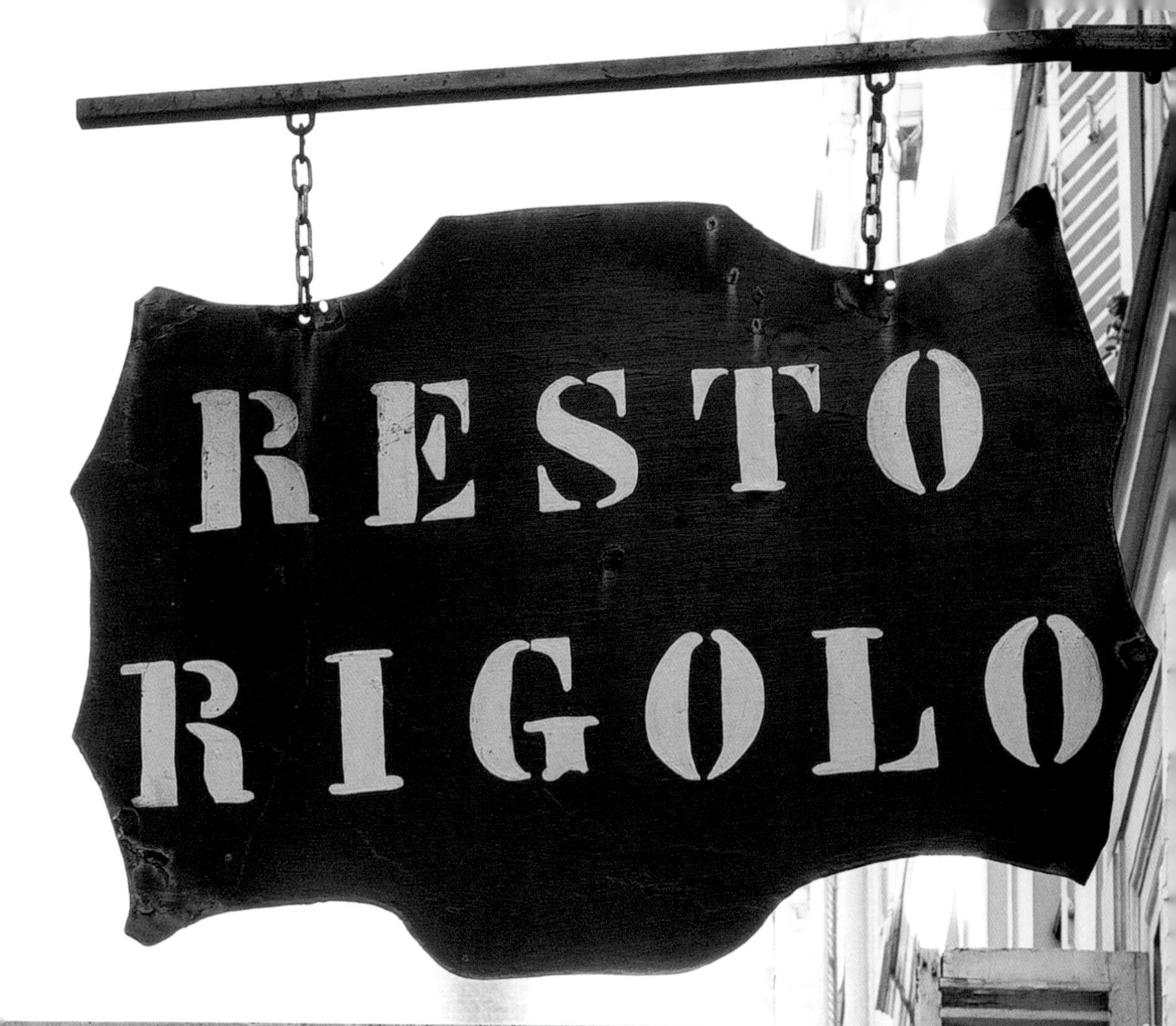
RESTO
RIGOLO

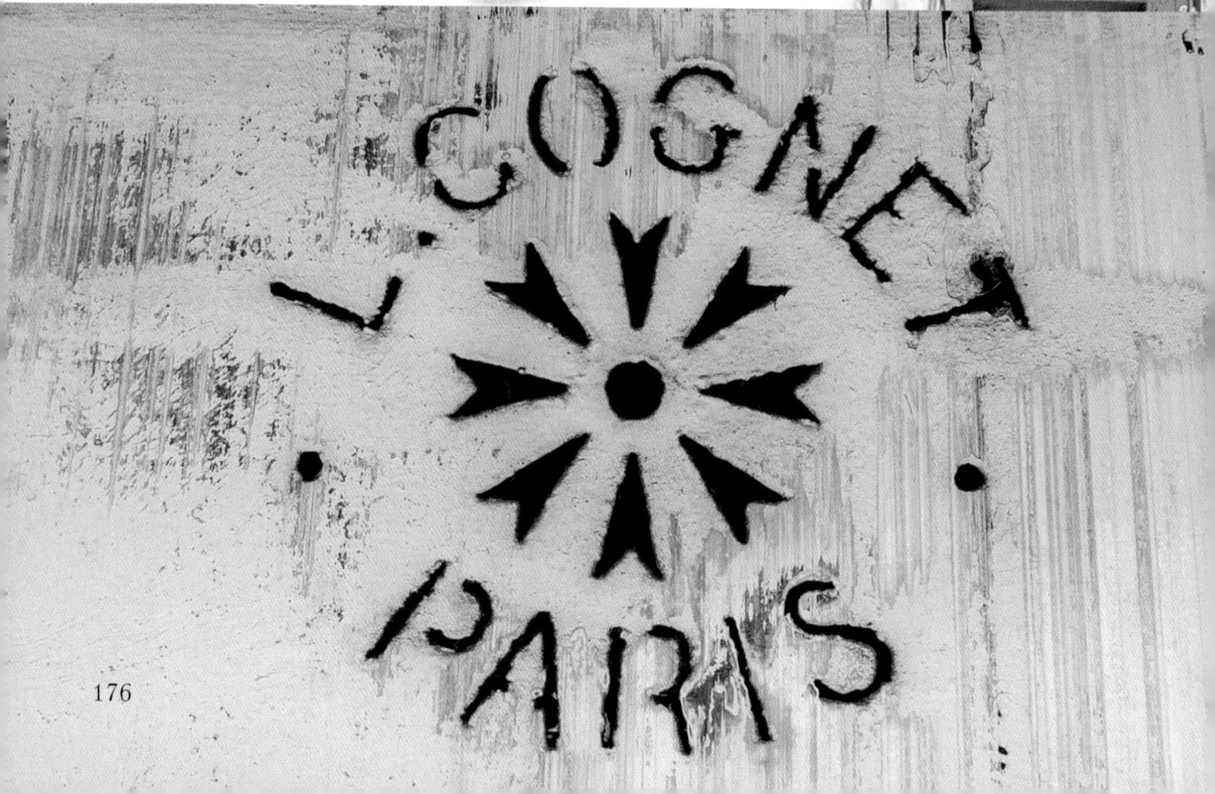
L COGNET
PARIS

ART D'AUJOURD'HU

SÉRIE 3, NUMÉRO DOUBLE 3 ET 4, 64 PAGES, FÉVRIER-MARS 1952, PRIX : 500 FRS

LE GRAPHISME ET L'AR

178

CADRAN

N°14

Patricia Roc, jeune vedette du cinéma angla
(voir page 30)

LISEZ DANS CE NUMÉRO :

LES PORTES DE L'ENFER *par John Berkeley*

UN ANGLAIS EN RUSSIE *par John Parker, M.P.*

LE MANNEQUIN PAR TROP HORRIBLE *par Gerald Kersh*

10frs.

DINEZ EN PLEIN AIR CHEZ

DROUANT
AU BOIS DE BOULOGNE
PAVILLON ROYAL

ORCHESTRE M. DE SWETSCHIN

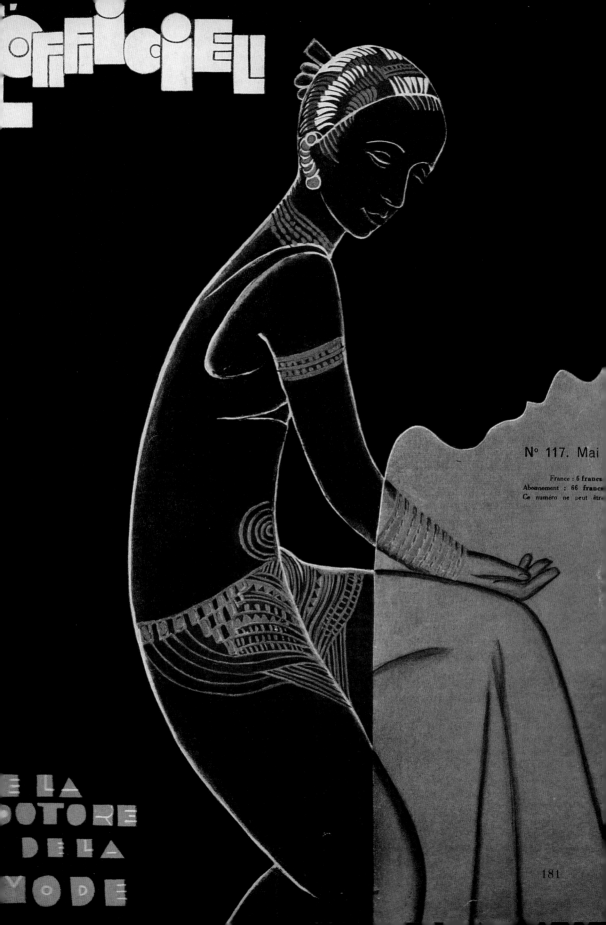

L'OFFICIEL

N° 117. Mai

France : 6 francs
Abonnement : 66 francs
Ce numéro ne peut être

E LA

OTORE DE LA MODE

181

L'ASSIETTE AU BEURRE

Qu'est-ce que que c'est?

PAR

Georges Meunier

N° 58. — 10 Mai 1902   40 centimes.

182

contre le Soleil

étui à lunettes fixé à la carosserie

jL DÉPOSÉE

toujours là, sous la main, pour protéger

AU
BUCHERON

AU
BÛ
CHERON

10 rue de
rivoli
PARIS

10 rue de rivoli PARIS

157. Magazine cover for *Arts et Métiers Graphique*, designed by Mazenod, Paris, 1937.

158–9. Metal stencil masks for Bodoni-style letters, *c.* 1915.

160–3. Enamel kitchen storage jars, *c.* 1920s.

164–5. Didot-style stencils, made from original stencil mask, 1920s.

166–7. Bifur type specimen pages, designed by A. M. Cassandre, Deberny & Peignot, Paris, 1939.

168. Fashion magazine advertisement for Setilose, 1937.

169. Packaging for Café Extra, *c.* 1939.

170–1. Deco lettering from *La Lettre artistique et moderne* by Draim, Monrocq frères, Paris, 1932.

172–3. Stencil woodchip pieces for unknown game, date unknown (collection of David Cohn).

174–7. Métro and shop signs, Paris (photographed by Louise Fili).

178. Magazine cover for *Art d'aujourd'hui: Le graphisme et l'art*, by Fernand Léger, 1952.

179. Magazine cover for *Cadran*, date unknown.

180. Advertisement for Drouant au Bois de Boulogne restaurant, 1928 (courtesy David Levine).

181. Magazine cover for *L'Officiel*, designed by Jean Dunand, May 1931.

182. Magazine cover for *L'Assiette au beurre*, designed by Georges Jeunier, May 1902.

183. Advertisement for Contre Le Soleil sunglasses, *c.* 1928.

184–5. Catalog for Au Bûcheron, Paris, *c.* 1932.

186. "Ananas" metal stencil, *c.* 1940s.

ITALIAN

STENCIL LETTERS WERE TOOLS OF POWER AND PROPAGANDA IN ITALY. Cadres of Fascist youth stenciled Mussolini's motivational sayings on walls throughout the country during the 1920s and '30s, and phrases such as, "it is better to live one day as a lion than one hundred years as a sheep," were part of an official graffiti campaign to rally the people behind Il Duce. His words were intended to project an improvisational appearance, which stencil letters accomplished so well. Lasting much longer than printed posters, stencils were an effective means of reinforcing the dictator's cult.

But the practice derived from an already existing tradition of stenciling everything from objects in the home to street signs. Stenciled variations of Bodoni and Didot date back to Napoleon's occupation of Venice in the late eighteenth century. Today, its wayfinding system gives the city its unique and graphic character, and the uniform street signs and locators (pp. 194–9), known as *nizioletti* for the white backgrounds on which they were painted, are visible on virtually every building and passageway. The stencil aesthetic can also be seen in the rest of the country: metal signs, hung from storefronts, contain the randomly occurring telltale breaks in letters, which allow for greater eye-catching appeal (pp. 189–93).

In the early twentieth century, the radical Futurists were enthusiastic users of stencil typefaces, appropriating vintage faces and designing newer ones based on modern styles for their manifestos. Although stencil is the opposite of a mechanical face, its application on machines in factories gave it a certain cachet. For these designers, the classification of type known as Didone, characterized by a strong contrast of thick and thin lines, represented the machine age. Italian foundries such as S. A. Xilografia Internazionale produced some exquisite examples of stencil derivatives, including the Tunisi series (p. 230), which was bold and spikey. Braggadocio, designed by W. A. Woolley for Monotype in 1930, imitated Paul Renner's Futura Black. Stencil was popularized, and it was inevitable that Italian avant-garde design would be integrated into mainstream advertisements and posters in an art deco style.

191

ROOMS

ARCHIE'S

FARM

HOTEL
LA FORCOLA

ACIA

AL VAPORETTO

←——————————→

VOLTO SANTO

CAMP

DEL T

PONTE DE LE
BECARIE

PARROCCHIA
S. SILVESTRO

ELLO

INTOR

CALLE DE LE VELE

318

CAMPIELLO DE LA CHIESA

324

2283

1648

4216	4209
4215	4210
4214	4211
4213	4212

CAMPIELLO DEL BOTER

CAMPO S. SOFIA

PARROCCHIA DI S.ZACCARIA

PONTE S.LORENZO

CORTE
ROMANO
BARBARO

RIVETTA

CAMPO
S. CANZIAN

IIIª Mostra Marinara d'Arte

PROMOSSA DALLA

LEGA NAVALE ITALIANA

PRESID. ONORARIO S.E. BENITO MVSSOLINI

OTTOBRE 1929 VIII ROMA PALAZZO DELLE
NOVEMBRE ESPOSIZIONI

RIDVZIONI FERROVIARIE

PARAGON DI STILE

ABCDEFGHIJKLM
NOPQRSTUUXYZ

ABCDEFGI
JKLMNOPQ
RSTUVWXY

abcdefg Z hiklmno
pqr stuvwxyz
1234567890

per voi.... per la vostra casa

LA RINASCENTE

carlo baragiola

SULLE ORME DI ROMA

(STUDIO SU L'AFRICA CENTRALE)

(Un naturale paesaggio africano presso le sorgenti del Congo)

editoriale "ARTE e STORIA" milano

Ettore Petrolini

Gastone

ONORJ

" A me m'ha rovinato la gue

La scala d'oro

UTET

La scala d'oro

Serie IVª
per i
ragazzi
i anni 9

N° 4

UTET

Il romanzo di Renardo

narrato da **Fernando Palazzi**
illustrato da **Guxtavino**

Flomart

MARCA DEPOSITATA

BIANCO DOLCE 900,

Domenico Florio Martinez & C
Marsala

RASSEGNA MENSILE

DIRETTA DA PRIAMO BRUNAZZI

2 lire

ANNO XII - N. 6

GIUGNO 1923 - VI

Scena Illustrata

Direttore : PILADE POLLAZZI

RIVISTA QUINDICINALE

Firenze, 1-15 Novembre 1935-XIV

Fascicolo doppio (21-22)
La Rivista esce ai primi d'ogni mese in fascicoli doppi.

-ARS-

Scena Illustrata

Direttore: PILADE POLLAZZI

Firenze, 1-15 Febbraio 1934 - XII

Fascicolo doppio (3-4) — Prezzo L. 3,50

La Rivista esce ai primi d'ogni mese, in fascicoli doppi.

Il conte di montecristo

EDIZIONI
MESSAGGERIE
MUSICALI

Grandi film illustrat

UOMINI

EDIZIONE TECNICA SPECIALE

ESCE UNA VOLTA AL MESE
32 PAGINE ILLUSTRATE   L. 2

Milano, 15 ottobre 1936-XIV - Anno III, N
Spedizione in abbonamento Pos
Direzione e Amministrazio
Milano - Via M. Aurelio, 6 - Telef. 286-

SOMMARIO

219

Torrone Biscotti Gelati

ROMA! LUCE DI CIVILTA' RINNOVATA DALL' ERA FASCIST[A]

ROMA! VOCE D' INCITAMENTO A SEMPRE PIU' OSARE

QUADERNO DI

NATURA

ANNO VI - N.4 - 30 APRILE 1933 (XI) - PREZZO L.8 - C.C.P.

MATERIALI CERAMICI PER
IMPIANTI SANITARI MODERN

NITOR

Società
Anonima
Materiali
Refrattari · MILANO

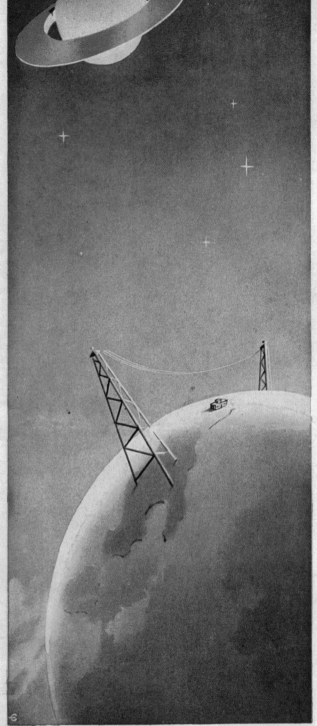

SOMMARIO

ANNO IV - N. 10-11 · OTTOBRE-NOVEMBRE 1932-XI

BOLLETTINO
PHILIPS RADIO

C. POSTALE

PERIODICO MENSILE

226

AUTOMOBILE CLUB DI PARMA
VIII° CAMPIONATO PROVINCIALE AUTOMOBILISTICO
17 MAGGIO IX°
ERBERTO CARBONI 1930

Cic. 25 - Classe B-p

Serie TUNISI

Cic. 30 - Classe C-g

189–93. Stenciled storefront signs, Rome (photographs by Louise Fili).

194–9. Stenciled street signs and numbers, Venice (photographs by Louise Fili).

200. Advertisement for Officine Galileo, 1941.

201. Program cover for *La Mostra Nazionale di Floricoltura*, designed by Mario Puppo, date unknown (courtesy David Levine).

202. Magazine advertisement for Institut de Beauté, *c.* 1932.

203. Poster for *La Mostra Marinara d'Arte*, designed by Latini, 1929.

204. Stencil letterforms from type specimen books, 1928–32.

205. Magazine advertisement for La Rinascente department store, 1933.

206. Cover for *Lunario delle muse 1932* almanac, designed by Santi, 1932.

207. Book cover for *Sulle orme di Roma*, Editoriale Arte & Storia, Rome, 1934.

208. Book cover for *Gastone*, designed by Onor, Cappelli Editore, Padua, 1932.

209. Book cover for *Nel Veneto e nel Fango*, designed by Schidani, Impresa Editoriale Italiana, Milan, 1931.

210–11. Book cover for *Il romanzo di Renardo*, illustrated by Gustavino, Unione Tipografica–Editrice Torinese, Turin, 1935.

212. Point-of-purchase display for Domenico Florio Martinez & Co., Marsala, *c.* 1940.

213. Magazine cover for *Rannegna*, designed by Erberto Carboni, 1928.

214. Magazine cover for *Scena Illustrata*, Florence, November 1935.

215. Magazine cover for *Scena Illustrata*, Florence, February 1934.

216. Poster for Ramazzotti, designed by Gino Boccasile, 1933.

217. Magazine cover for *Grand Hotel*, designed by Mariani, *c.* 1948.

218. Magazine cover for *Grandi Film Illustrati*, *c.* 1940.

219. Magazine cover for *Uomini*, illustrated by Marcello Dudovich, October 1931.

220. (top) Point-of-purchase display for *biscotti al torrone*, *c.* 1938; (bottom) cover for *Quaderno*, designed by Rigorini, *c.* 1939.

221. Magazine cover for *Natura*, illustrated by Paolo Garretto, April 1933.

222. Advertisement for Società Anonima Materiali Refrattari, Milan, *c.* 1938.

223. Newsletter cover for *Bollettino*, Philips Radio, Milan, October–November 1932.

224–5. Packaging for Panettoni Amati, Milan, date unknown (copy based on original).

226–7. (left to right) Handpainted disks with marks for Fascist organizations, 1937; metal stencil masks, *c.* 1948; advertising fan for Calzature Casella, *c.* 1938.

228. Magazine cover for *La Borsa*, designed by Mario Sironi, 1936.

229. Poster for Automobile Club di Parma, designed by Erberto Carboni, 1930.

230. Tunisi typeface specimen from S. A. Xilografia Internazionale, *c.* 1933.

SPANISH

A RT DECO GRAPHICS EXPLODED IN SPAIN DURING THE LATE 1920S and early '30s with a dialect all their own, and stencil type was part of the explosion. Propagandists, graphic designers, and printers used it with relative frequency to communicate political, social, and commercial messages to the public. Stencil, and what might be called "faux stencil," were among the array of modernistic and futuristic styles that defined the Spanish graphic persona.

The faux-stencil mannerism was a favorite among designers. It employed stencil characteristics, but was not entirely the real thing. Spanish Deco letterers issued many stencil-derived variations, and were not shy about playfully tarting up and hybridizing otherwise classic thick and thin faces. Futura Black and its imitators were also in high demand. Type shops either custom-made or imported typefaces from Germany and France, and these stencils, used directly from the typecase without added embellishment, were bold attention-grabbers, especially for magazine advertisements, which required a modish look.

Display types and letters such as Mar and Oriente (pp. 236–7) and Primavera and Intex were much too fussy to be actually made into a stencil. But the "stencilization" of these letters (the detached serifs, seemingly separate, yet touching, vertical strokes, and multiple vertical spaces) enabled designers to have a range of distinctive effects, although they were not always endowed with the most legible formal traits.

Spain fostered its share of stencil classicists, too. The thirty custom wine registration marks (pp. 246–56) by an anonymous designer, possibly a student, in about 1920, were mostly handdrawn and collected in a personal scrapbook, along with non-stenciled alternatives. Although a few of the examples are sans-serif with hints of moderne styling, including "Toro Tigre" (pp. 248–9) and "El Globo" (p. 250), the majority of examples are stencilized bifurcated Tuscan letters and other serif faces. That stencil was favored says something about how the marks were printed on the bottles or corks, as well as revealing a taste for slightly eccentric typographic hijinks.

DIETARIO

1932

✦

ALMACENES JORBA

PU-
BLI-
CI-
DAD.

Espumoso del

RHIN

Año 1903

IMPORTADO POR BERNARDO SANCHEZ, S. A. · BILBAO

EL ENCANTO DEL MAR

En cada pedazo de historia vibra la voz del mar. Los pueblos que se hacen sordos a ella, que a las aguas marinas dan la espalda y emprenden su ruta tierra adentro, envejecen pronto. En la caricia de las olas o en el rugir de sus latigazos de espuma, hay dinamismo y juventud. Así lo comprendió el hombre en los umbrales de la civilización, que en el mar hallaba nuevas energías para la dura lucha por la vida. Fenicios y griegos llevaron en sus naves la riqueza y la cultura, y Roma fué poderosa cuando dominó en el mar. El esplendor de los pueblos es el esplendor de sus naves, es el magnífico poema de las aguas. A orillas del mar se levantan las grandes ciudades del mundo, surgen los hombres de aventura, se forjan nuevas quimeras y viven y mueren los capitanes de leyenda, gentes que no conocen ni admiten imposibles, que ven en cada ola una invitación a la vida, a la vida alegre del trabajo, de la aventura y de la lucha. Y los que no sueñan tanto, los que no ambicionan ir más allá del horizonte unido a las aguas, con sus barcas menudas al mar le arrancan tesoros de vida. Cada uno interpreta la canción del mar a su modo; la melodía es eterna e infinita. ¡Oh mar latino, el mar de las gestas de los pueblos heraldos de la civilización! ¡Atlántico bravío, ruta de aventuras de Colón y sus compañeros en el sueño dorado de las Indias! ¡Inmenso Pacífico, explorado un día por naves de España!... Vuestras aguas son historia, historia viva, que palpita en cada época, en cada generación, en cada nave que se hunde en las profundidades inmensas del horizonte lejano... La historia de todos los países, en sus períodos imperiales, fecunda sus brillantes episodios en las gestas de las naves, mares a dentro, en busca de grandezas, con afanes de gloria hacia la inmortalidad.

HUGO WIEGERK

ORIENTE

EDICIONES
NUEVA ASIA

Una Tez de I

Una Nueva Idea Asombros
En los Polvos de Tocad

Experiencias científicas han revelado una maner
y fácil para que los polvos permanezcan adheridos
todo el día. Este maravilloso descubrimiento p
todas las mujeres que conserven la tez fresca y
—sin la menor huella de brillantez—durante una r
tera, bailando en salas muy caldeadas. El ingredi
c sigue esta asombrosa diferencia se llama Esp
Crema y los derechos patentados para emplearla fu
quiridos por Tokalón con una suma enorme. Por co
te, los Polvos Tokalón, los famosos polvos parisie
los únicos polvos genuinos con espuma de crema.

una tez
que la llu
viento má
to no pue
truir.

Las triu
de todos
cursos de
desde hace
años han e
polvos.

La señ
Universo
secreto de
200.000 pe
reina de b

Los o
ahora la f

238

tas. 200.000

cilla
cutis
te a
ante
e en-
que
de
ad-
uien-
son
ran
ecta
o el
len-
des-

oras
on-
leza
nos

eado esta clase especial de

Yolanda Pereira, Miss
, declara: «Este sencillo
leza me permitió ganar
y me ayudó a ser elegida
del mundo.»

ctos Tokalón contienen
a espuma de crema.

INDUSTRIAS

TEXTILES

SELECT

CASA JOSEP SERRA

PER A EQUIPS DE NUVIA I LLENCERIA FINA
ES LA PRIMERA
Creacions propies
LA COL·LECCIÓ MES IMPORTANT I
MODERNA EN JOCS DE TAULA I LLIT

Rbla de Catalunya 79 xamfrà València Teléfon 71396

246

VINO MALAGA SECO SUPERIOR QUEVEDO

LAS TRES ANCORAS

Sr. RÓMULO BOSCH Y ALSINA & Cª
GARANTIDO
Marca Registrada.

BODEGA DE Sn. FELIX

VINO NAVARRO SUPERIOR

R.B.

DURANGO

247

MARCA

TORO

MARCA

TIGRE

249

VINO NAVARRO SUPERIOR

MARCA REGISTRADA

VICTORIA

UNICOS RECEPTORES B. Fernandez & Cª HABANA

BF & Cª
HABANA
CUBA

VINO LEGÍTIMO DE ALELLA

La CODORNIZ

MARCA
REGISTRADA

CORTINA

VILAFRANCA DEL PANADÉS

252

VINOS DE MARCA

ROMULO BOSCH

Premiados con medallas de oro
y otras distinciones en las
Exposiciones de

BARCELONA - 1888
PARIS —— 1900
TURIN —— 1902
VIENA —— 1903
ATENAS —— 1904

VINOS ESPECIALES

MACLIONI Y SASSO

MARCA DOS LEONES

VINO M SECO EXTRA

PINGO

Unicos Introductores
STORACE Y Cia
MONTEVIDEO

253

VINO MÁLAGA SECO SUPERIOR

CATALUÑA

REGISTRADA

VINO LEGÍTIMO
DE
MISA
R. BOSCH

FLOR DEL PRIORATO
R. BÓSCH

255

VINO TINTO ESCOGIDO
LA VERBENA
DE LA

VINO TINTO SUPERIOR DE MESA
EL
R. BOSCH

VALDEPEÑAS MOMPÓ
R. BOSCH Y ALSINA

MOSCATEL SUPERIOR
DEL PRIORATO

VINO SUPERIOR
SAN IGNACIO
GARANTIZADO

LAS
DOS
LUNAS
MARTIN FALK BARCELONA

256

233. Cover for Almacenes Jorba diary, 1932.

234–7. Publicidad type specimen pages, 1930.

238–9. Advertisement for face powder, Tokalon, *c.* 1934.

240–1. Publicidad type specimen page, detail, 1930.

242–3. Advertisement for women's accessories, Lorens, Valencia, *c.* 1934.

244. Advertisement for "Select" women's undergarments, Casa Josep Serra, Valencia, *c.* 1934.

245. Advertisement for Sedes textiles, *c.* 1934.

246–56. Scrapbook of handdrawn identity marks for various wines and oils, date unknown.

GERMAN

JUGENDSTIL, DECO, AND MODERNISM WERE THE DOMINANT GRAPHIC
styles in Germany in the nineteenth and early twentieth centuries—all had
stenciled alphabets available as templates or fonts. With amateurs and professionals alike engaged in the fashionable pastime of stenciling ornamental letters and
monograms onto materials of all kinds, a huge variety of custom and standard
lettering styles in the form of copper plates were produced and became as widely
available as conventional unadorned stencils. The former had an Arts and Crafts
purpose, while the latter were produced for more utilitarian aims.

Stencil letters were frequently employed in mass-market advertisements,
posters, magazines, and books, providing them with two very distinct identities—
casually stylish on the one hand, symbolic or metaphoric on the other. The logo for
Dame magazine (p. 276) from the early 1920s is an example of the former. The
witty playfulness is seen in the lack of uniform channels between letters—it is
deliberately haphazard, but clearly legible. A magazine advertisement from 1950
(p. 277) illustrates the second type. Here, the word "Kaffee" is a direct reference
to the stenciled letters on the burlap bags the coffee beans were transported in.

The art of stencil lettering was exemplified by Futura Black, designed by
German type master Paul Renner and released by Bauer Type Foundry in 1936.
It remains the quintessential Modernist typeface, and at the time was promoted
by type foundries as "cubistic," or modern. Futura Black looked nothing like the
original Futura, but was nonetheless a member of an extended type family that
helped define the graphic style of the era. It also became the model on which
many other geometric stencil typefaces the world over were based.

Stencils enabled designers the opportunity—indeed, the freedom—to experi-
ment with form, and break typographic rules in the bargain. The covers of
Gebrauchsgraphik (pp. 278–9) showed unique fat and condensed variants of
Futura Black, and a distinct curvilinear version that illustrated the versatility of
geometric stencils. On the surface, the stencil method appeared to offer limited
outcomes, but German designers revealed it to possess endless eclectic possibilities.

1000

TAKTE

TANZ

BAND 7

MERKENTHALER MONOGRAMM MODERN

№ 914

MUSTER GESCH.

SCHUTZ VAEKE

F.Z.

ges geschützt

64

DIRECTOIR-STIL

F ♂

102

F.Z.

F.Z.

F.Z.

F.Z.

F.Z.

F.Z.

F.Z.

FZ

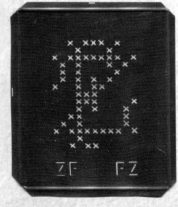

ZF   FZ

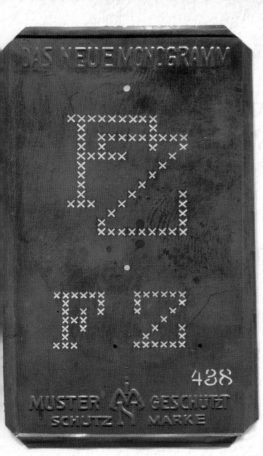

DAS NEUE MONOGRAMM

438

MUSTER GESCHÜTZT
SCHUTZ MARKE

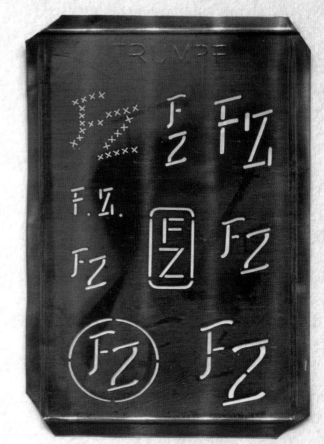

TRUMPE

MEISTER THALERS
"KÜNSTLER-KREUZSTICH"

N° 004

MUSTER GESCHÜTZT · SCHUTZ MARKE

MUSTER GESCH. · SCHUTZ MARKE

JUGEND

FZ 912

MUSTER GESCHÜTZT

F.Z.

F.Z.

F.Z.

F.Z.

F.Z.

F.Z.

F.Z.

F.Z.

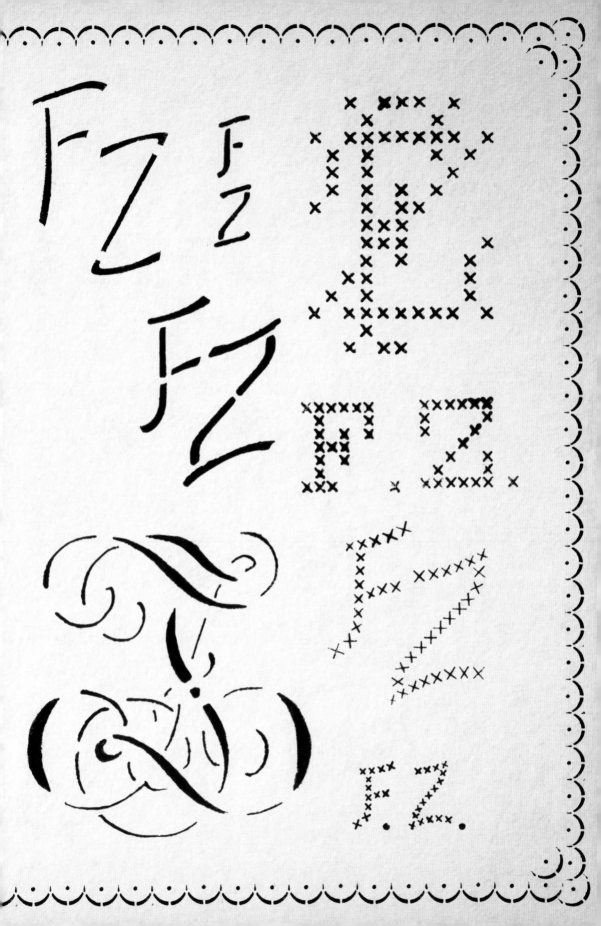

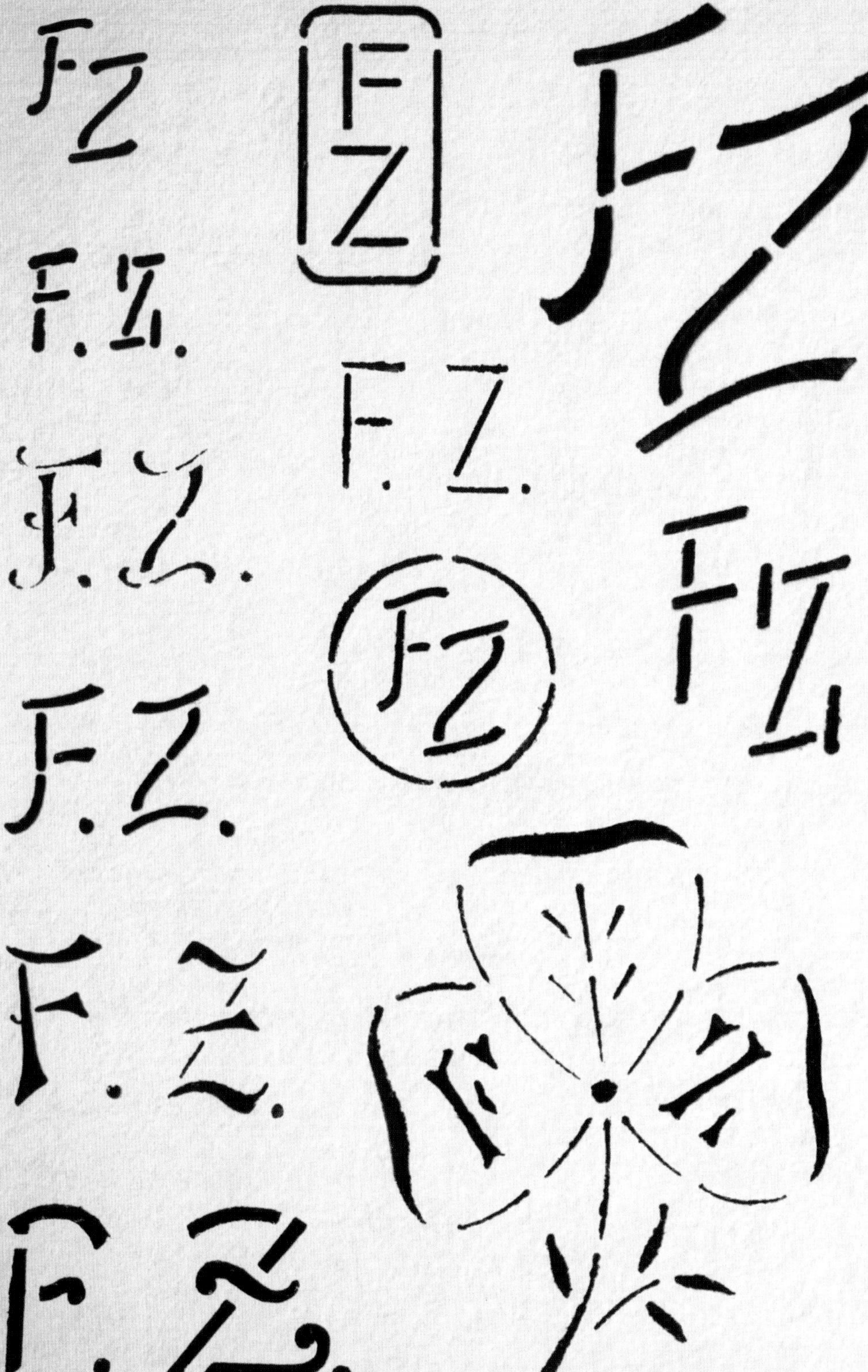

269

a b c d e f g h i j k

l m n o p q r f s t

u v w x y z

This stencil type is produced with typographical material (Brass Rule) and can, as shown by specimens 1, 2 and 3, be made in varying heights and thicknesses.

a b c a b c

BIOMALZ
HILFT

311

ABCDE
EUROPA
ABCDEFGHIKLMS
OPQRSTUVWXYZ

abcdefghijklmno
pqrstuvwxyz
ABCDEFGHIJKLMN
OPQRSTUVWXYZ

ABCDEFGHIJKLMN
OPQRSTUVWXYZ

LIAM O'FLAHERTY

DIE

BESTIE

ERWACHT

S. FISCHER VERLAG

A. M. FREY

DIE PFLASTER-KÄSTEN

EIN FELDSANITÄTS-ROMAN

G SALTER

11.—20. TAUSEND

GUSTAV KIEPENHEUER VERLAG

Die Herzen
gewinnen

KHASANA

Lippenstift
Wangenrot

M 1.50, 1.- und -.50

Dame

Neues Heft!

KAFFEE

JULI 1928 JULY

GEBRAUCHSGRAPHIK

MONATSSCHRIFT ZUR FÖRDERUNG KÜNSTLERISCHER REKLAME

INTERNATIONAL ADVERTISING ART

MONTHLY MAGAZINE FOR PROMOTING ART IN ADVERTISING

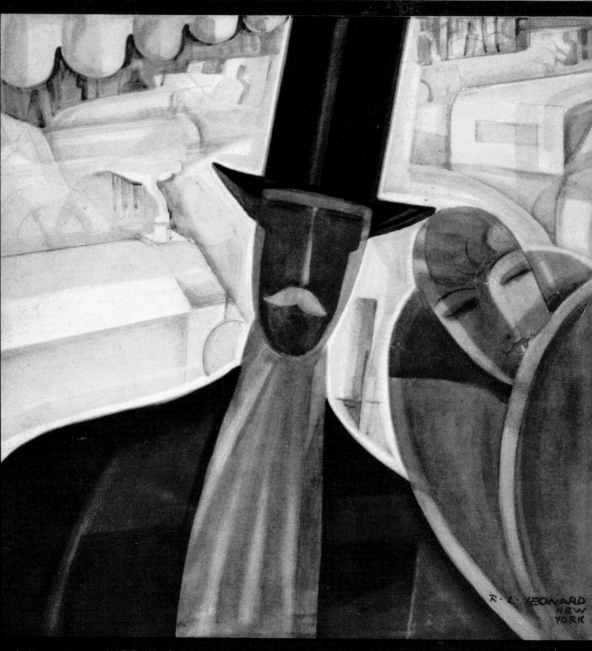

R·L·LEONARD
NEW
YORK

HERAUSGEBER·PROF·H·K·FRENZEL·EDITOR

PHÖNIX ILLUSTRATIONSDRUCK UND VERLAG G·M·B·H BERLIN SW

Allein-Vertreter für die Vereinigten
Staaten von Nordamerika u. Kanada
THE BOOK SERVICE COMPANY
15 EAST 40 STREET NEW YORK CITY U·S·A
Sole Representative for the United
States of America and Canada

GEBRAUCHSGRAPHIK
INTERNATIONAL · ADVERTISING ART

FEBRUAR 1931 FEBRUARY

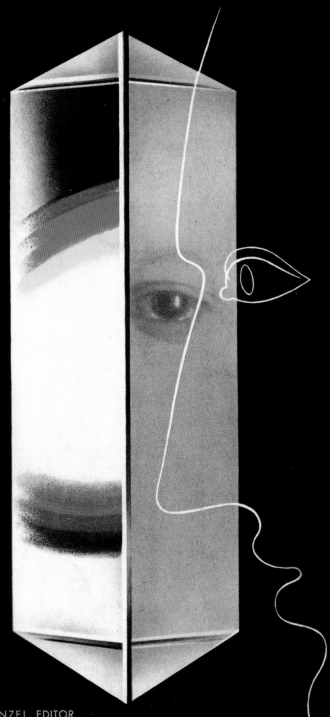

JEAN
CARLU

HERAUSGEBER: PROF. H. K. FRENZEL, EDITOR
PHÖNIX ILLUSTRATIONSDRUCK UND VERLAG GMBH., BERLIN SW 61,
BELLE · ALLIANCE · PLATZ 7 · 8

ALLEINVERTRETER FÜR DIE VEREINIGTEN STAATEN VON NORD-AMERIKA UND KANADA:
THE BOOK SERVICE COMPANY. 15 EAST 40TH STREET, NEW YORK CITY USA.
SOLE REPRESENTATIVE FOR THE UNITED STATES OF AMERICA AND CANADA

1930

GUT NEU JAHR

FAMILIE WERNER

CARL HAENSEL

ZWIEMANN

Ein Roman aus der großen Industriewelt.
Höchst fesselnde Einblicke in den Aufbau, die
internationalen Hintergründe und familiären
Komponenten eines modernen Chemie-Trusts.
Mit souveränem Blick wird das Zusammen-
spiel von Wirtschaft und Politik entwickelt
und in den einzelnen Menschen werden
Kräfte unserer Zeit gegeneinandergestellt.

EUGEN DIEDERICHS VERLAG · JENA

WEINGUTSBESITZER-UND-WEINGROSSHANDLUNG
HEINR. ECKEL & Cie
ÜNCHEN-DEIDES-
EIM-RUPPERTS-
BERG

FUTURA

SCHMUCK

BAUERSCHE ■
GIESSEREI
FRANKFURT-M

LEIPZIG BERLIN BARCELONA MADRID BILBAO SEVILLA

corps 20   1 Min. 10,5 kg

Arbre généalogique

CRISTAL DE ROCHE

corps 24   1 Min. 12 kg

Horario de trenes

MAGNIFICENCIA

corps 28   1 Min. 14 kg

Die Rundschau

SCHLOSSHOF

corps 36   1 Min. 16 kg

Importance

ANTIMONY

corps 48   1 Min. 22 kg

Zeefdruk

DEINING

corps 60   1 Min. 26 kg

Banana

CROCE

corps 72/60   1 Min. 26 kg

Storm

BAUM

corps 84/72   1 Min. 25 kg

Puoti

REKI

WIR PFLEGEN DEN
QUALITÄTSDRUCK
IN ALLEN DRUCKVERFAHREN

SCHIRMER
&.MAHLAU
FRANKFURT A/MAIN

BESONDERE ABTEILUNG FÜR KLISCHEEN.
HERSTELLUNG UND OFFSETÜBERTRAGUNGEN.

bittrof

EGON ERWIN KISCH

BEEHRT SICH
DARZUBIETEN:

PARADIES
AMERIKA

ERICH REISS VERLAG

G. SALTER

die **Bayerische Volkszeitung** in Nürnberg,

Stil und Aufmachung haben sie nicht nur für Nürnberg, sondern auch für Bayerns Regierungspartei repräsentativ gemacht. Die BV ist nicht nur Zeitspiegel im Kampf um die letzte Minute, sondern auch das größte und maßgebende Organ für das katholische Nordbayern. Umstände, die zugleich den Anzeigenteil der BV wertvoller machen, denn die redaktionelle Leistung bietet ja überhaupt erst die Grundlage für die Wirkungsmöglichkeit des Anzeigenteils

Berliner Geschäftsstelle der BV:
Eugen Satmong, Berlin-Wilmersdorf, Tharandterstr. 5
Fernsprech-Nummer: H 7 Wilmersdorf 8472

BAD EMS
DAS HEILBAD

EMS

Modes
de
Sylvie Rose
30   30
Fournisseur
de la Cour

Otto
Gotha
Berlin
Kiel

IN DE DREY KONINGEN

Sam. Weller
Ship Broker

Vins
du
Rhin
et de
Hongrie

Arnold
Ladies
Taylor

ART
ancien et Moderne

1904

STAD VEURNE

·Prijskamp·
·Voor · het · Visschen·
·met · de · lijn·

Café

Harold Pym

Shoemaker

Tickets pour Vichy

Avis

W·C

W·C

Odéon

ARTUS
de Bretagne

Tous les Soirs

à 8 h. et ½

Lancelot
Sarah Bernhardt
Genièvre · Artus
Moreno
de Max

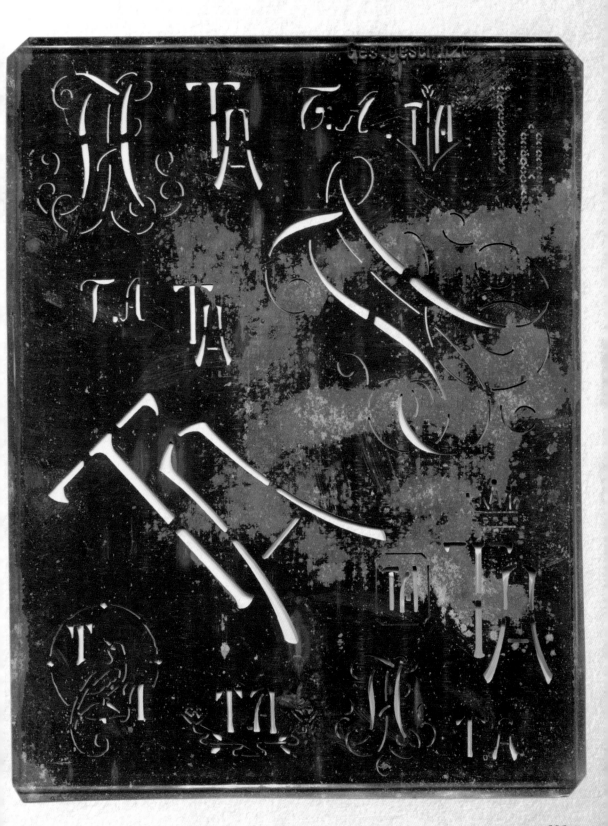

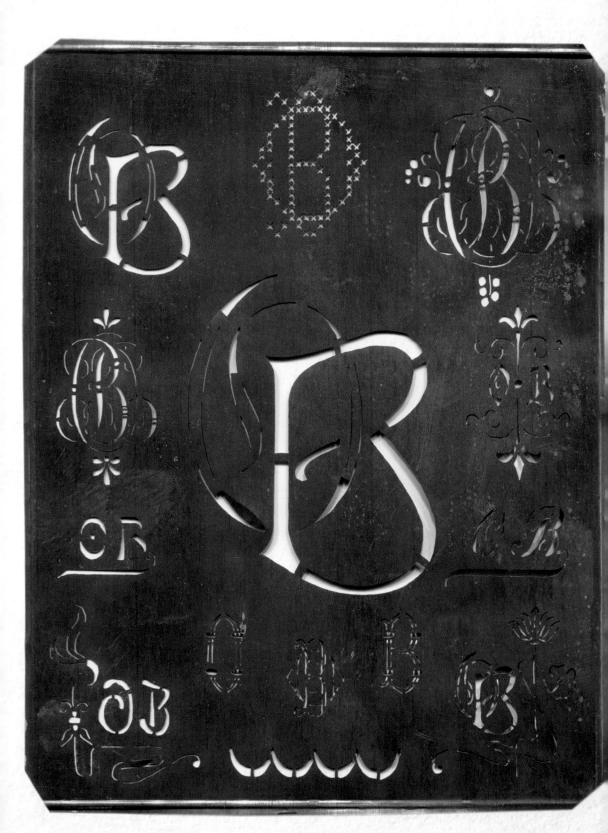

296

259. Cover for *1000 Takte Tanz*, sheet music booklet, designed by Herzig, *c.* 1937.

260–1. Jugendstil stencil masks for monograms and letters, *c.* 1900s.

262–5. Print iterations of Jugenstil stencil masks, *c.* 1900s.

266–9. Variations of stencils as logos and identity marks, 1930.

270. (top) Stencil lettering; (bottom) sketch from Herbert Hoffmann, ed., *Modern Lettering: Design and Application*, William Helbrun, New York, 1930.

271. Various stencil styles from Herbert Hoffmann, ed., *Modern Lettering: Design and Application*, William Helbrun, New York, 1930.

272. Book cover for *Die Bestie erwacht*, designed by George Salter, S. Fischer Verlag, Berlin, *c.* 1929.

273. Book cover for *Die Pflasterkästen*, designed by George Salter, Gustav Kiepenheuer Verlag, Berlin, date unknown.

274. Advertisement for Khasana cosmetics, 1930.

275. Advertisement for Das Echo newspaper, *c.* 1920s.

276. Magazine cover and poster for *Dame*, *c.* 1923.

277. Advertising poster for Kaffee, designed by Milti Nagl, 1950.

278. Magazine cover for *Gebrauchsgraphik*, illustration by R. L. Leonard, July 1928.

279. Magazine cover for *Gebrauchsgraphik*, illustration by Jean Carlu, February 1931.

280. "Gut Neu Jahr" card for Familie Werner, 1930.

281. "Winter in Bayern" travel/holiday brochure, *c.* 1933.

282. Book cover for *Zwiemann*, Eugen Diederichs Verlag, Jena, 1930.

283. Advertisement for Heinrich Eckel & Cie, Munich, 1928.

284. Futura Schmuck (decorations) specimen, Bauer Type Foundry, *c.* 1930.

285. Futura type specimen page, Bauer Type Foundry, *c.* 1930.

286. Advertisement for Schirmer & Mahlau, Frankfurt, designed by Max Bittrof, 1931.

287. Book cover for *Paradies Amerika*, designed by George Salter, Erich Reiss Verlag, Berlin, *c.* 1937.

288. Advertisement for *Die Bayerische Volkszeitung* newspaper, from *Die Reklame*, January 1933.

289. (top) Trademark for Deutsches Gut, date unknown; (bottom) "Bad Ems" title for a road map, 1930.

290. Advertisement for Hostmann-Steinberg, from *Gebrauchsgraphik* magazine, designed by Dobsky, June 1932.

291. Luggage label for Hotel Wilden Mann, Lucerne, *c.* 1925.

292–3. Various examples of Jugenstil lettering from a specimen book, *c.* 1910.

294–6. Masks for Jugendstil stencil monograms, *c.* 1900s.

DUTCH

S TENCILED ALPHABETS BLOSSOMED IN HOLLAND AFTER THE TURN
of the last century, nurtured by modern avant-garde experimentation. The
"stencilized" logo for *De Stijl #7* (p. 308), the radical journal of the art movement of the same name, was designed by Theo van Doesburg using horizontal
and vertical rectilinear shapes with spaces between them. Hendricus Theodorus
Wijdeveld, editor-in-chief of the progressive architecture and graphics magazine
Wendingen, designed his own variant of Futura Black, with accent on the curves.
He also created distinctive architectonic alphabets, such as the title page of the
catalog for the De Bijenkorf department store (p. 300), made to look like a stencil
printing with multiple masks.

But these were among the edgier examples designed for more rarefied media.
Dutch commercial typographers, fluent in the art of Deco styling, were just as
willing—indeed, happy—to become "stencilified." Original and stencil-influenced
typefaces were prominently used in mainstream advertisements, posters, and
magazines. They symbolized extreme modernity, but were perfect for popular
consumption. Some were drawn directly from Futura Black and used in such a
way as to add dimension to the page, other faces were customized with stencil
highlights in the Deco spirit.

Because stencil was such a playful medium to work with, eccentricity was
encouraged—as seen in the logo for *Germania* newsletter (p. 307), which plays
with the geometric quirks of the forms. A commonly promoted typographic trope
involved using large stenciled numerals for their eye-catching sculptural qualities. The stencil's popularity was contingent on the ongoing promotion of foundry
faces, which necessitated exposing designers to new ways of using them. The
trade journal *De Reclame* (pp. 302–3, 305) favored a variety of old and new typefaces, among them a fair share of stencils, which in turn appealed to trend-savvy
designers. Specifying any of the modern stencil typefaces in the 1920s and '30s
was the fashionable thing to do. Although the public was largely blind to type
nuances, they were nonetheless subconsciously aware of the symbolic cues.

PLUKT DE VRUCHTEN

DE PAPIERMOLEN

TIJDSCHRIFT VOOR DE GRAFISCHE VAKKEN

DE BIJENKORF
s Gravenhage

RADIO EXPRES

№ 43

8 October

IN DIT NUMMER:

Het voorhistorische kristaltoestel — Experimenteele
Televisie, Deel III — Hoogfrequentlampen zonder

PRIJS

25

11e JAARGANG No 14
5 APRIL 1932
RED. EN ADMINISTR.
HOFWIJCKSTR. 9, DEN HAAG

DE RECLAME

maart
1933

No. 22 - 31 MEI 1932
11e JAAR

Reclame

verschijnt elke week

RED. EN ADMIN. HOFWIJCKSTR. 9. DEN HAAG

Canal
TOUR

Binder
STERK

No. 6 ● 6e JAARGANG
● MAART 1936 ●

Germania

ORGAAN AMSTERDAMSE SPORTVERENIGING „GERMANIA"
OPGERICHT 29 MEI 1927 - KONINKL. GOEDGEKEURD 10 SEPT. 1929

Redactie: P. Suurendonk - A. Teunissen - J. Berghammer ● Redactie en admin.-adres: G. de Beer - Saenredamstraat 12 huis

No. 2554 Corps 24   12 A, 27 a   Minimum 7 **Kg.**

Reise in Persien
Soll und Haben
FROHE STUNDEN
Bark De Zetkast
MEUBELEN

No. 2557 Corps 48   5 A, 12 a   Minimum 11 Kg.

Election

DE STIJL

MAANDBLAD VOOR DE MO-
DERNE BEELDENDE VAKKEN
REDACTIE THEO VAN DOES-
BURG MET MEDEWERKING
VAN VOORNAME BINNEN- EN
BUITENLANDSCHE KUNSTE-
NAARS. UITGAVE X. HARMS
TIEPEN TE DELFT IN 1917.

299. Brochure cover for *De Papiermolen*, designed by Jan Handig, 1933.

300. Catalog title page for De Bijenkorf department store, designed by Hendricus Theodorus Wijdeveld, 1926.

301. Magazine cover for *Radio Express*, October 1938.

302. Magazine cover for *De Reclame*, April 1932.

303. Magazine cover for *De Reclame*, March 1933.

304. Advertisement for KLM, designed by Machteld den Hertog, *c.* 1932.

305. Magazine cover for *De Reclame*, May 1932.

306. Corps typeface specimen sheet, 1930.

307. (top) Masthead for *Germania* newspaper, March 1936; (bottom) Corps typeface specimen sheet, 1930.

308. Masthead for *De Stijl* journal, designed by Vilmos Huszár and Theo van Doesburg, 1917.

BRITISH

HISTORICALLY, THE ROLE OF STENCIL LETTERING IN BRITAIN may be minor, but it has significance as an essential part of the nation's mercantile tradition. England itself had long been a seafaring trading country, with generations of imports and exports passing through its great shipping ports. Packing crates, wooden boxes, and burlap bags filled with goods were routinely tagged with stenciled images and letters—branding, by any other name.

It was not until the 1910s that stencil emerged from being a purely utilitarian vernacular into more of an art form, when a more liberal appreciation among designers of stencils acquired aesthetic acceptance. In the early part of the twentieth century, English designers were often caught between two strong typographic currents—Modernist minimalism and Art Deco ornamentation. Stencil typefaces were the bridge between fashion and ideology, and by the late 1920s, stencil and faux-stencil type were firmly entrenched as a symbol of British modernity.

One of Futura Black's many derivators, Transit, designed by Jan Tschichold in 1931, became popular among type-users for its streamlined kinetic quality. It was the graphic equivalent of an aerodynamic automobile, a symbol of the present future. Other echoes of Futura Black included dozens of one-offs, including the headline for an advertisement for the Raymond & Whitcomb travel agency (p. 319), with a new twist—overlapping transparent letters, a virtual impossibility if this had really been stenciled instead of drawn in the manner of one.

Not all stencils are equal. The title for *The Mysterious Universe* (pp. 312–13), for example, which contains a few letters with stencil traits, is injected with a lethal dose of Art Deco decorative conceit. Similarly, the masthead for *Advertising Display* magazine (p. 323), while eye-catching, combines stencil characteristics with novelty tricks to its detriment. With stencil lettering, simpler is better—just look at the clean lines of the word "Picasso" (p. 318) on an exhibition poster and the solid angularity of "Spicers 'W. King'" (pp. 316–17), which imbue each typeface with power and pleasure.

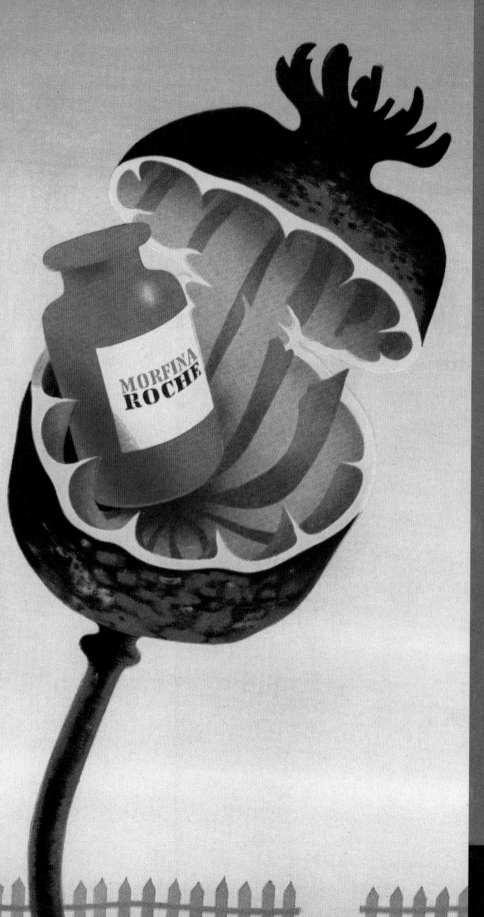

THE
MYSTERIO
UNIVERSI

JEANS

MACMILLA

THE
MYSTERIOUS
UNIVERSE

by
Sir JAMES JEANS

SPIC

'W. I

ERS
ING'

NOON POST

THE ZWEMMER GALLERY

A NEW EUROPE

MOTORING ABROAD

RAYMOND AND WHITCOMB CO

SIGNAL PRESS

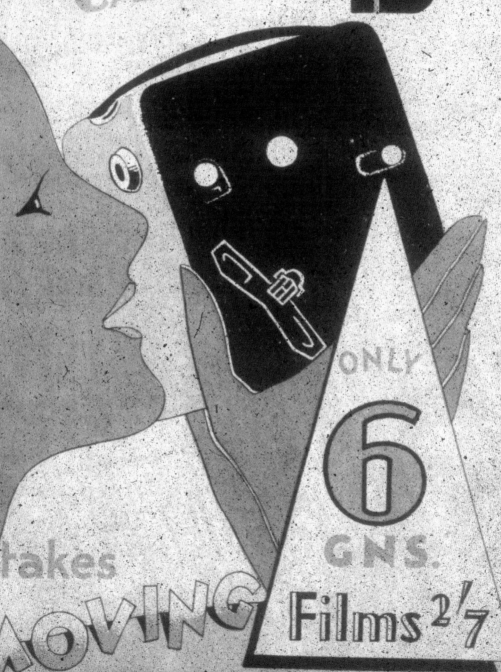

THE NEW 6/8 EDITION
Cheerio
BY W.H.KITCHEN
AND J.WESTGAR
ADDITIONAL LYR
BY MICHAEL CA
FEATURED by MAX MILLER
in
GEORGE BLACK's NEW SHOW
APPLE-SAUC
PRICE 1/
2ND PRIZE WINNING SONG IN THE
NEWS CHRONICLE SONG COMPETITION
PETER MAURICE

ADVERTISING DISPLAY.

MAY 1928

1 shilling

E.McK.K.

311. Transito typeface specimen sheet, designed by Jan Tschichold, Amsterdam Type Foundry, 1931.

312–13. (left) Advertisement for Roche, designed by Lewitt-Him, 1937; (right) book cover for *The Mysterious Universe*, Macmillan, London, 1930.

314–15. (top) Stencil metal mask; (bottom) print iteration, date unknown.

316–17. Advertisement for Spicers "W. King", detail, 1949.

318. (top) Masthead for *Noon* Post newspaper, 1948; (bottom) advertisement for *Picasso*, Zwemmer Gallery, London, 1936.

319. "Motoring Abroad" advertisement for Raymond & Whitcomb Co., London, 1928.

320. Advertisement for Shenval Press, London, designed by Imre Reiner, 1949.

321. Advertisement for Pathéscope, date unknown.

322. Advertisement for a stage show, in *Cheerio*, 1940.

323. Magazine cover for *Advertising Display*, designed by E. McKnight Kauffer, May 1928.

324. Merchant's sign and coat of arms for Stumpp *c.* 1938.

EASTERN·EUROPE

THE CZECH AVANT-GARDE ENJOYED WHAT APPEARED TO BE A LOVE affair with stencil type. If Karel Teige's cultural magazine *ReD* (pp. 338–9) is any indication, it was definitely a requited romance. For his design of the magazine's distinctive covers, Teige used a customized stencil face for the masthead, often in conjunction with standard typewriter type. As these are the two most vernacular typographic styles, the combination signaled a rejection of conventional magazine design in favor of a new ad-hoc approach.

The *ReD* covers avoided the clichés, and were not anarchic like many other avant-garde journals. The combination of these two faces and the overarching dominance of the stencil masthead expressed informality—and informality was modern. Stencil type does not make much of an appearance elsewhere in *ReD*, but it does in Teige's other work. In fact, avant-gardists in Poland, Hungary, and elsewhere in Eastern Europe were influenced by the Bauhaus, De Stijl, and Constructivism, in which stencil is found in abundance. So it is not surprising that Teige and other likeminded designers employed variations of stencil lettering in their work, often in a symbolic, left-leaning way.

The symbolism inherent in stencil lettering was not, however, monolithic. Its representation shifted according to how and for what it was used. The left-wing embraced it as a proletarian typeface, a factory worker's face. Avant-garde artists (who were likely to be on the left) engaged with stencil as representative of future advances in technology, and intense shifts in art, culture, and politics. For the business world, it was an empty vessel that was stylish enough to reach contemporary audiences with any message when used in eye-catching advertisements.

Throughout Eastern Europe, subtle changes were made to Paul Renner's original Futura Black. The Hungarian poster maquets reproduced in *Gebrauchsgraphik* for coffee, butter, and beer (pp. 344–7) show a preference for stencil that works in contrast with the airbrushed imagery, drawing the eye as much to the words as to the images. There was a strong decorative side to stencil, as well, which blended a folk sensibility with a modernistic lettering form.

ART

TEMPERY

SUWALSKI

BUSZEK

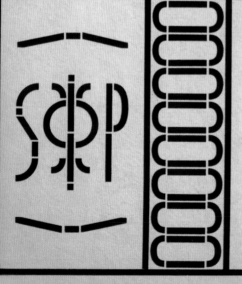

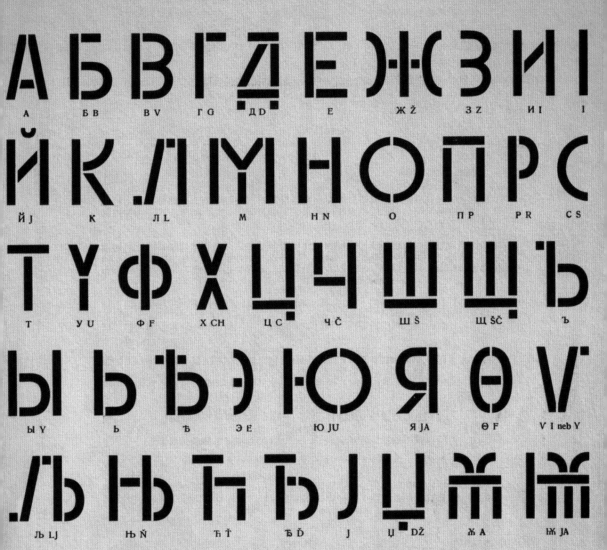

AAAAAAAAABB
CCCDDDEEEFF
GGHHIJJKKK
LLLMMMMMNN
NNOOPPPQRRS
STTUUUUUVVV
IJUWWXXYYZ&
1234567890
(.,:„"!§?';-)

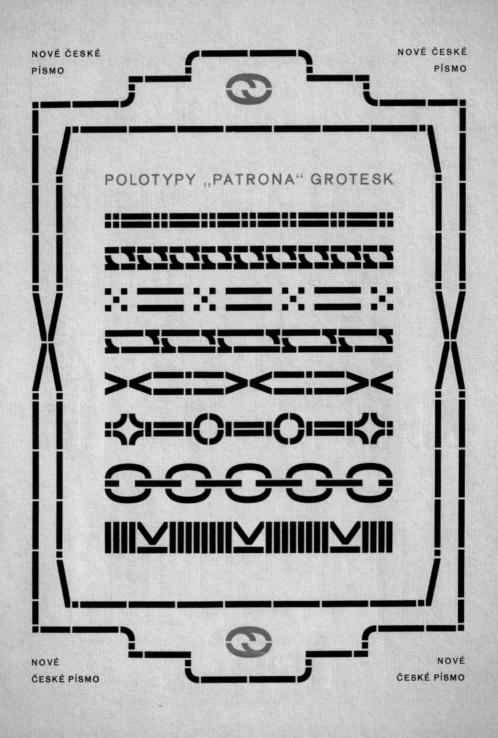

POLOTYPY „PATRONA" GROTESK

POLOTYPY

PATRONA

POSKYTUJÍ MOŽNOST SESTAVITI NEJVĚTŠÍ POČET TYPŮ,

STEJNÝCH, UŽŠÍCH NEBO ŠIRŠÍCH.

PATRONA

JE NOVÉ ORIGINÁLNÍ ČESKÉ PÍSMO.

Z POLOTYPŮ

ПАТРОНА

SÁZÍ SE RUŠTINA, SRBŠTINA I BULHARŠTINA.

ZÁKONEM CHRÁNĚNO – GESETZLICH GESCHÜTZT

MARQUE DÉPOSÉE – REGISTERED

POLOTYPY

PATRONA
GROTESK

KRESLIL V. KÁNSKÝ

CELOU

ŘADU PÍSEM

MOŽNO SESTAVITI

Z JEDINÉHO STUPNĚ NÁMI VYDANÝCH POLOTYPŮ „PATRONA" GROTESKU:

4 CICERO „PATRONA" GROTESK, 4 CICERO „PATRONA" GROTESK RUSKÉ
8 CICERO „PATRONA" GROTESK, 8 CICERO „PATRONA" GROTESK RUSKÉ
I JEDNOTLIVÁ SLOVA OBYČEJNÁ NEBO RUSKÁ I V JINÝCH STUPNÍCH

JEDINÉ PÍSMO HODÍCÍ SE K SESTAVOVÁNÍ A K TISKU BEZ POUŽITÍ STEREOTYPIE

A DALŠÍ ÚPRAVY.

NOVINKA

DODÁVÁ

SLEVÁRNA
PÍSEM

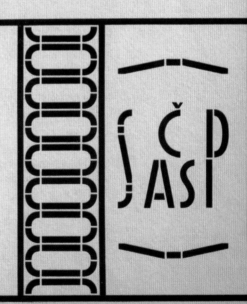

ČESKÁ AKCIOVÁ SPOLEČNOST

V PRAZE II., SOKOLSKÁ TŘÍDA Č. 25 n

TELEFON 376-32

SEZNAM

POLOTYPŮ „PATRONA" GROTESK

1 minimum ca 16 kg. Cena za 1 kg Kč 40'—.

Figury č. 8, 9, 12, 13, 14, 15 jsou opatřeny výřezy.

———

ZÁKONEM CHRÁNĚNO — GESETZLICH GESCHÜTZT

MARQUE DÉPOSÉE — REGISTERED

POLOTYPY

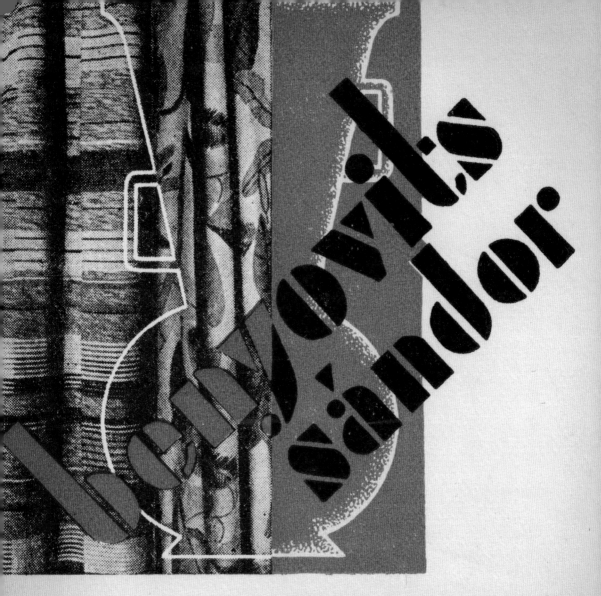

MODERN LAKÁS

TEXTIL

IPARMŰVÉSZET

BUDAPEST, IV, VÁCI UCCA 12

TELEFON 82-6-35

FUTURA

PÍSMO DNEŠNÍ DOBY

Zde není rozhodujícím přizpůsobení liter strojnímu výkonu, nýbrž to, že písmo samo vykazuje jasný a určitý ráz stroje. Vzhledem k principu samotnému, zdálo by se býti nejvýše zajímavým pokusem. Ve skutečnosti jest však více, jest pokusem velice šťastným; v pravdě jest také mnohem více, než nový bezvýznamný strojový výrobek, neboť jest písmem značného významu. - Jest mnoho groteskových písem, jež technickým zjednodušením rázu písmu Futura hodně se přibližují, avšak žádné z nich, v klasické čistotě obrazu sazby, se mu nevyrovná. Pozoruhodné při tomto písmu také jest, že není jen pokusem změny liter do abstraktních forem, nýbrž že obraz písma vzdor těmto formám působí jako celek nejvýš harmonicky a neunavuje. (Hermann Herrigel v časopise »Kunstwart«)

Bauersche Giesserei

FRANKFURT A·M · BARCELONA · NEW YORK

ZÁSTUPCE PRO ČESKOSLOVENSKOU REPUBLIKU

B. FR. ZRNKA · PRAHA II

wiedza

nr 10

1932

i życie

cena zł. 1.50

R⅁D

4

měsíčník pro moderní kulturu

Jacques Lipchitz

**spolupracovníci:
collaborateurs:
mitarbeiter:**

Hans Arp, J. Babel,
Willi Baumeister, Konstantin Biebl, Pierre
Albert Birot, C. Brancussi, Le Corbusier &
Pierre Jeanneret, Max
Ernst, J. Fučík, L. Feininger, J. Honzl, Paul
Klee, Lautréamont, E.
Linhart, Jacques Lipchitz, El. Lissickij,
Jiří Mařánek, Pierre
Minet, Moholy-Nagy, Murayama, F. Picabia, E.
Piscator, V. J. Průša,
Man Ray, Z. Rossmann,
J. Seifert, Ives Tanguy, V. Tatlin, L. Theremin, Tristan Tzara,
B. Václavek, J. Voskovec, F. C. Weiskopf

leden 1928

6 K

8

ročník 2.

duben 1929

odeon

RED

měsíčník pro moderní kulturu

rediguje karel teige

Pro titulní montáž ke knize P. Girard: Poznejte lépe srdce žen. (Knížky pro potěšení)

karel teige (1928): frontispice

foto

film

typo

PAX

HOMINIBUS BONAE

VOLUNTATIS

GRAFIKA

5

341

Grafika Polska

3

czasopismo poświęcone

SZTUCE GRAFICZNEJ

t gronowski 1927

AVIATIKA

A
MAGYAR AERO
SZÖVETSÉG

ÉS
TAGEGYESÜLETEINEK
HIVATALOS LAPJA

343

II. évf. 4. szám   Ára 80 fillér   1931 április

meinl

kávé

bortnyik

Berény

SZARVAS SZAPPAN

Hutter

hutter

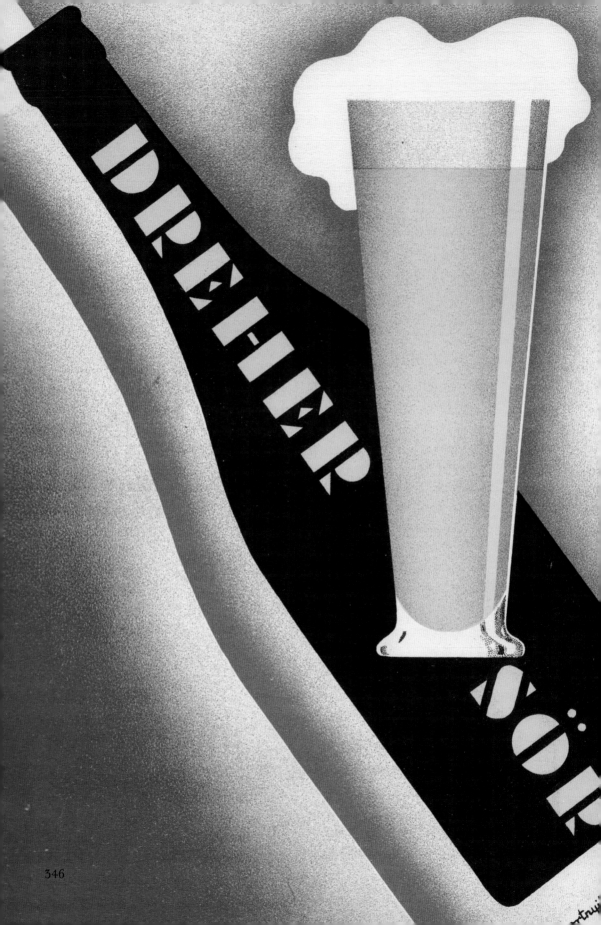

Franck

a kávédarálóval

bortnyik

348

327. Advertisement for art supplies, designed by W. Suwalski, Poland, *c.* 1930.

328–34. Polotypy (Patrona Grotesque) typeface specimen sheet with language variations, Czechoslovakia, 1930s.

335. Trade card for Sándor Benyovits, Hungary, *c.* 1932.

336. Advertisement for Futura, in *Typographica* magazine, Czechoslovakia, 1933.

337. Magazine cover for *Wiedza i Zycie*, Poland, 1932.

338. Magazine cover for *ReD*, designed by Karel Teige, Czechoslovakia, 1928.

339. Magazine cover for *ReD*, designed by Karel Teige, Czechoslovakia, 1929.

340. Magazine cover for *Grafika 5*, Poland, date unknown.

341. Advertisement for art supplies, Poland, 1932.

342. Magazine cover for *Grafika Polska 3*, designed by Tadeusz Gronowski, Poland, 1937.

343. Magazine cover for *Aviatika*, Hungary, April 1934.

344. Advertisement for Meinl coffee, designed by Sándor Bortnyik, Hungary, *c.* 1930.

345. Advertisement for Hutter soap, designed by Róbert Berény, Hungary, *c.* 1930.

346. Advertisement for Dreher beer, designed by Sándor Bortnyik, Hungary, *c.* 1930.

347. Advertisement for Franck coffee, designed by Sándor Bortnyik, Hungary, *c.* 1930.

348. New Year's greeting card for a printing company, Hungary, 1931.

Abbe, Dorothy, *Stenciled Ornament and Illustration: A Demonstration of William Addison Dwiggins' Method of Book Decoration and Other Uses of the Stencil* (Hingham, Massachusetts: Puterschein-Hingham, 1979).

Annenberg, Maurice, *Type Foundries of America and their Catalogs* (1975; New Castle, Delaware: Oak Knoll Press, 1994).

Cabarga, Leslie, *Progressive German Graphics: 1900–1937* (San Francisco: Chronicle Books, 1994).

Carlyle, Paul, and Guy Oring, *Letters and Lettering* (New York and London: McGraw-Hill, 1943).

DeNoon, Christopher, *Posters of the WPA* (Los Angeles: The Wheatley Press, 1987).

Duvall, Edward J., *Modern Sign Painting* (New York: Fredrick J. Drake & Co., 1949).

Fraser, James, and Steven Heller, *The Malik Verlag, 1916–1947: Berlin, Prague, New York* (New York: Goethe House, 1984).

Heller, Steven, *Merz to Emigré and Beyond: Avant-Garde Magazine Design of the Twentieth Century* (London: Phaidon Press, 2003).

Heller, Steven, and Seymour Chwast, *Graphic Style: From Victorian to Post-modern* (New York: Harry N. Abrams, 1988).

Heller, Steven, and Louise Fili, *Deco Type: Stylish Alphabets of the '20s and '30s* (San Francisco: Chronicle Books, 1997).

———, *Typology: Type Design from the Victorian Era to the Digital Age* (San Francisco: Chronicle Books, 1999).

Hoffmann, Herbert, ed., *Modern Lettering: Design and Application* (New York: William Helbrun, c. 1930).

Hollis, Richard, *Graphic Design: A Concise History* (London: Thames & Hudson, 1994).

Hutchings, R. S., *A Manual of Decorated Typefaces* (London: Cory, Adams & Mackay, 1965).

Kelly, Rob Roy, *American Wood Type, 1828–1900: Notes on the Evolution of Decorated and Large Types* (New York: Da Capo Press, 1969).

Lewis, John, *Printed Ephemera: The Changing Uses of Type and Letterforms in English and American Printing* (Woodbridge, Suffolk: Antique Collectors Club, 1990).

———, *Typography: Design and Practice* (London: Barrie & Jenkins, 1978).

———, *The Twentieth Century Book: Its Illustration and Design* (London: Studio Vista Limited, 1967).

Lista, Giovanni, *Le livre futuriste* (Modena and Paris: Éditions Panini, 1984).

McLean, Ruari, *Jan Tschichold: Typographer* (London: Lund Humphries, 1975).

———, *Victorian Book Design and Colour Printing* (London: Faber & Faber, 1963).

———, *Pictorial Alphabets* (London: Studio Vista, 1969).

Müller-Brockmann, Josef, *A History of Visual Communication* (Teufen, Switzerland: Verlag Arthur Niggli, 1971).

Poynor, Rick, *Typographica* (New York: Princeton Architectural Press, 2001).

Purvis, Alston W., and Martijn F. Le Coultre, *Graphic Design 20th Century* (New York: Princeton Architectural Press, 2003).

Schriften-Atlas (Berlin: H. Berthold, 1914).

Specimen Book and Catalogue 1923 (Jersey City, New Jersey: American Type Founders Company, 1923).

Spécimen général (Paris: Fonderie Deberny et Peignot, 1926).

Specimens of Printing Types (New York: George Bruces' Son & Co., 1882).

Spencer, Herbert, ed., *The Liberated Page* (San Francisco: Bedford Press, 1987).

———, *Pioneers of Modern Typography* (New York: Hastings House, 1969).

Thompson, Bradbury, *The Art of Graphic Design* (New Haven and London: Yale University Press, 1988).

Welo, Samuel, *Practical Lettering: Modern and Foreign* (Chicago: Frederick J. Drake & Co., 1930).

Wood Letter (Sheffield: Stephenson, Blake & Co., 1959).

MUCH GRATITUDE GOES TO LUCAS DIETRICH AND ELAIN MCALPINE at Thames & Hudson for their continued enthusiastic support of this and our earlier books.

Thanks to Spencer Charles and Kelly Thorn at Louise Fili Ltd for their excellent work on the layouts and cover.

The book's content is mostly from our own collections, but would not be possible without tips from dealers and friends, and friends who are dealers.

Thanks to David Levine at travelbrochuregraphics.com for his contributions.

Thanks to Seymour Chwast for loaning us a beautiful stencil, and to David Cohn for supplying us with remarkable treasures.   S.H. *&* L.F.